# ADVENTURES IN
# PALEONTOLOGY

## 36 CLASSROOM FOSSIL ACTIVITIES

# ADVENTURES IN PALEONTOLOGY

## 36 CLASSROOM FOSSIL ACTIVITIES

By Thor Hansen and Irwin Slesnick

Illustrations by D.W. Miller

NATIONAL SCIENCE TEACHERS ASSOCIATION

Claire Reinburg, Director
Judy Cusick, Senior Editor
Andrew Cocke, Associate Editor
Betty Smith, Associate Editor
Robin Allan, Book Acquisitions Coordinator

PRINTING AND PRODUCTION Catherine Lorrain, Director
 Nguyet Tran, Assistant Production Manager
 Jack Parker, Electronic Prepress Technician
 Will Thomas, Jr., Art Director

NATIONAL SCIENCE TEACHERS ASSOCIATION
Gerald F. Wheeler, Executive Director
David Beacom, Publisher

LIBRARY OF CONGRESS CATALOGING-IN-PUBLICATION DATA

Hansen, Thor A.
  Adventures in paleontology : 36 classroom fossil activities / by Thor
Hansen and Irwin Slesnick ; illustrations by D.W. Miller.
    p. cm.
  Includes bibliographical references.
  ISBN-13: 978-0-87355-272-1
  1. Paleontology--Study and teaching (Middle school)--Activity
programs.    I. Slesnick, Irwin L.  II. Title.
QE715.H36 2006
560.71'2--dc22
                        2006003510

NSTA is committed to publishing material that promotes the best in inquiry-based science education. However, conditions of actual use may vary, and the safety procedures and practices described in this book are intended to serve only as a guide. Additional precautionary measures may be required. NSTA and the authors do not warrant or represent that the procedures and practices in this book meet any safety code or standard of federal, state, or local regulations. NSTA and the authors disclaim any liability for personal injury or damage to property arising out of or relating to the use of this book, including any of the recommendations, instructions, or materials contained therein.

SCiLINKS. *Featuring sciLINKS ®—connecting text and the internet. Up-to-the-minute online content, classroom ideas, and other materials are just a click away.*

Figures 2.12, 2.16, 2.17, 2.28, 2.41, and 7.3 adapted from *Dinosaurs,* by D. Norman, J. Sibbick, D. Blagden, and D. Nicholls. Random House, 1996.

Figure 6.9 adapted from a photo in *Dinosaurs, An Illustrated History,* by E. H. Colbert, Hammond World, 1983.

# TABLE OF CONTENTS

# TABLE OF CONTENTS

At one point or another, it seems like all students are interested in paleontology. Wonderful extinct animals like dinosaurs excite the imagination like almost nothing else. Once you have the students' interest, you will find that a study of paleontology provides avenues of exploration into a wide variety of foundational sciences such as biology, geology, chemistry, physics, and astronomy (See Table 1). Paleontology is also an excellent way to teach to the National Science Education Standards (NRC 1996), and all of the activities in this book are aligned with one or more of the Science Content Standards for grades 5–8 (See Table 2). We use an active hands-on approach because that is the best way to learn. A great teacher I know has a sign above his desk that reads, "If they hear it, they will forget. If they see it, they will remember. If they do it, they will learn." It is the philosophy of this book that learning through hands-on activities is the best way to integrate new knowledge.

The activities in this book are targeted primarily at teachers and students in grades 5–8 because studies have shown that these grades are a crossroads for students in regard to science. At this age many children decide whether or not they like science based on school activities, and unfortunately most decide that they do not. For example, the Third International Mathematics and Science Study (1999) showed that whereas only one country outperforms U.S. students in math and science at fourth-grade level, nine countries do so by eighth grade. We believe that engaging, inquiry-based, hands-on activities represent a vital way to capture the minds of these students. Though middle school grades are the primary audience for these activities, many of them have been used with both younger and older audiences. For example, I (Thor Hansen) regularly incorporate many of the activities in this book in my college classrooms with only minor modifications.

This book comprises 36 different activities organized into 9 chapters. Chapter 1 (How Do Fossils Form?) discusses the ways that organisms become fossils and illustrates these concepts with activities that simulate fossil-making processes. Chapter 2 (What Can You Learn From Fossils?) explores what fossils can teach us about ancient organisms and also includes an explanation and activities using scientific inquiry. Chapter 3 (Mass Extinctions and Meteor Collisions With Earth) discusses the recent links that have been made between meteor and asteroid impacts on Earth and the demise of animals like the dinosaurs. Activities in this chapter include how to find real meteorites in your own yard and modeling the effects of meteorite impacts. Chapter 4 (How Are Fossils Collected?) describes some ways that fossils are found and prepared and guides the reader through the steps of preparing real fossil specimens. In Chapter 5 (How Can You Tell the Age of Earth?), students will make their own model for demonstrating the great age of Earth and the relative durations of important time intervals. Chapter 6 (How Did Dinosaurs Evolve?) explores the methods of cladistics and facilitates an understanding of evolution through active learning. Chapter 7 (Diversity, Classification, and Taxonomy) places fossils in the contexts of their distribution on the globe and how we name them and quantify their communities. Chapters 8 (Fossils in Society) and 9 (Fossils in Art) look at fossils from a humanistic perspective.

Major scientific disciplines covered in each activity in this book. Number under "Activity" corresponds to chapter and activity number, e.g. "1-1" refers to Chapter 1, Activity 1.

Abbreviations:
Biol = Biology, Chem = Chemistry, Math = Mathematics, Phys = Physics, Geol = Geology, Astro = Astronomy, Ecol = Ecology, Evol = Evolution, Sci Meth = Scientific Method, Lng/Art = Language and Art.

| Activity | Biol | Chem | Math | Phys | Geol | Astro | Ecol | Evol | Sci Meth | Lng/Art |
|----------|------|------|------|------|------|-------|------|------|----------|---------|
| 1-1 | | | | | X | | | | | |
| 1-2 | X | | | | | | | | | |
| 1-3 | | | | | X | | | | | |
| 1-4 | | X | | | X | | | | | |
| 1-5 | | | | | X | | | | | |
| 1-6 | | | | | X | | | | | |
| 1-7 | X | X | | | | | | | | |
| 2-1 | | | | | | | | | X | |
| 2-2 | X | | | | | | | | | |
| 2-3 | X | | | | | | | | | X |
| 2-4 | X | | | | | | | | | |
| 2-5 | X | | X | X | | | | | | |
| 2-6 | X | | | | | | | | | |
| 2-7 | | | | | X | | X | | | |
| 2-8 | X | | | | | | X | | | |
| 2-9 | X | | | | | | X | | X | |
| 3-1 | | X | | | | X | | | | |
| 3-2 | | | X | X | | X | | | | |
| 3-3 | | | X | | | X | | | | |
| 3-4 | | | X | | | X | | | | |
| 4-1 | X | | | | X | | | | | |
| 4-2 | | | | | X | | | | | |
| 4-3 | X | | | | | | | | | |
| 5-1 | | | | | X | | | | | |
| 6-1 | X | | | | | | | X | | |
| 6-2 | X | | | | | | | X | | |
| 6-3 | | | | | | | | X | | |
| 6-4 | | | | | | | | X | | |
| 7-1 | | | | | X | | | | | X |
| 7-2 | | | | | | | | | | X |
| 7-3 | | | | | X | | | | | |
| 7-4 | | | X | | | | X | | | |
| 8-1 | | X | | | X | | | | | |
| 8-2 | | | | | X | | | | | |
| 9-1 | | | | | | | | | | X |
| 9-2 | | | | | | | | | | X |

Alignment of activities in this book to the National Science Education Standards (National Research Council, 1996). Columns refer to Content Standards A–G for grades 5–8. Number under "Activity" corresponds to chapter and activity number, e.g. "1-1" refers to Chapter 1, Activity 1. Abbreviations: Pers = Personal, Perspect = Perspectives.

| Activity | A Science as Inquiry | B Physical Science | C Life Science | D Earth & Space Science | E Science & Technology | F Science in Pers and Social Perspect | G History & Nature of Science |
|---|---|---|---|---|---|---|---|
| 1-1 | | | | X | | | |
| 1-2 | | | X | | | | |
| 1-3 | | | | X | | | |
| 1-4 | | X | | X | | | |
| 1-5 | | | | X | | | |
| 1-6 | | | | X | | | |
| 1-7 | | X | X | X | | | |
| 2-1 | X | | | | | | X |
| 2-2 | | | X | X | | | |
| 2-3 | | | X | X | | | X |
| 2-4 | X | | X | X | | | |
| 2-5 | X | | X | X | | | |
| 2-6 | X | X | X | | | | X |
| 2-7 | | | X | X | | | |
| 2-8 | | | X | X | | | |
| 2-9 | X | | X | X | | | X |
| 3-1 | | | | X | | X | |
| 3-2 | | X | | X | | X | |
| 3-3 | | X | | X | | X | |
| 3-4 | | X | | X | | X | |
| 4-1 | | | X | X | | | |
| 4-2 | | | | X | | | |
| 4-3 | | | X | X | | | |
| 5-1 | | | | X | | | |
| 6-1 | X | | X | X | | | |
| 6-2 | | | X | X | | | |
| 6-3 | X | | X | X | | | X |
| 6-4 | | | X | X | | | |
| 7-1 | | | X | X | | | |
| 7-2 | | | X | X | | | |
| 7-3 | | | X | X | | | |
| 7-4 | | | X | | | | |
| 8-1 | | | | X | | X | |
| 8-2 | | | X | X | | | |
| 9-1 | | | | | | X | |
| 9-2 | | | | | | X | |

# How Do Fossils Form?

A fossil is any evidence of an ancient organism. The remains of the body, such as bones, shells, leaf impressions, etc. are called body fossils. The evidence of animal activity, such as tracks, trails, and burrows, are called trace fossils. Body fossils can be preserved:

◆ In an unaltered state where the hard parts such as shell or bone are relatively unchanged. In exceptional cases the organism may be mummified, frozen, or preserved in amber.
◆ By carbonization. This is indicated by a black film on an impression of the organism such as a leaf. This black film is the organic residue of the organism after its other material is removed or replaced by the fossilization process.
◆ By permineralization. In this case, pores of the skeleton of the organism (such as bone or wood) are replaced with mineral. Most petrified wood is preserved in this manner.
◆ By replacement. Original shell or bone undergoes an atom-by-atom substitution with another mineral. Pyrite (fool's gold) is a common replacement mineral. The replaced fossil is usually a faithful replica of the original.
◆ By molds and casts. Here the original material dissolves leaving only impressions or infillings. Impressions of the interior or exterior of a fossil are molds. An infilling of the mold, so that an exact likeness of the organism is reproduced, is a cast.

SCI LINKS.
THE WORLD'S A CLICK AWAY

Topic: Fossils
Go to: www.scilinks.org
Code: AP001

## TEACHER'S NOTES:

### Making a mold and cast ........................................................................... CHAPTER 1, ACTIVITY 1
This is a real crowd pleaser. It takes about 45–60 minutes and is a little messy, but produces beautiful impressions that students will want to keep. Hand out cups and leaves (or other material to be used as "fossils" such as feathers or shells) and have the students put their name on the bottom of the cup. Mix a large batch of plaster of paris with water to a fairly thick consistency for the first filling of each cup. You or the students should half-fill each cup. While they are arranging their "fossils" on the surface, make another batch of plaster with which to cover the fossil and fill the cup. This pause will allow the initial filling to firm up a little. Fill the cups to the top and let them harden before you try to crack them open (they will feel very warm). When the plaster is hard, peel off the paper and break open the plaster at the line of the fossils. Some of the blocks will be breakable by hand. Others will need a sharp rap on a table edge or they can be opened with a chisel or nail and a hammer.

### Making a mold and cast of your teeth ....................................................... CHAPTER 1, ACTIVITY 2
This is a variation of activity 1 which students find fascinating. How often do you get to see the inside of your own mouth? With a razor blade or Exacto knife, carefully cut around each paper cup about 1/2 inch up from base. Make the incisions parallel to the lip and leave about 1/2 to 1 inch uncut, producing a "hinge." Hand out one to each student. While the students put the clay in the bottom of the cups and press their teeth into the clay, mix a batch of plaster of paris. The plaster should be a little thin so that it fills the cavities of their impressions. Make sure to let the plaster get good and hard before attempting to remove the clay because the points of the teeth will be fragile.

### Simulating permineralization ................................................................ CHAPTER 1, ACTIVITY 3
This activity produces a remarkably hard, rock-like "bone" out of an ordinary kitchen sponge. The sand it is buried in is also lightly cemented so that digging in it is like digging up a real fossil.

# Making a mold and cast

## MATERIALS:

- paper cup
- stirring stick
- plaster of paris
- hammer and nail
- large plastic bowl or tub for mixing plaster
- leaves, feathers, or other "fossils"

## Procedure:

Put your name on the bottom of the paper cup. Half fill the cup with plaster of paris. Press the leaf, feather, or other object you want "fossilized" onto surface of plaster. Do not submerge the leaves in the plaster, but make a layer sitting on the surface. The more of the surface that you cover with material the better. Wall-to-wall leaves (or feathers, or whatever) make it easier to split the plaster block later. Also if some of them touch the sides of the cup it makes it easier to see where the splitting point should be. Add plaster to near the top of the cup. Be careful as you pour the second layer of plaster. If the first layer is still very fluid, pouring the second layer may cause the two layers to mix and to jumble the leaves. You want the leaves to be on a flat surface, parallel to the table (perpendicular to the walls of the cup). For this reason, it is best to pour the first layer, lay on the leaves, and then wait a few minutes for the first layer to set a little before pouring the second layer. If you make the plaster fairly thick, it will set more quickly. After the plaster hardens (10–20 minutes, it will undergo a chemical reaction that produces heat), tear off the paper cup and use the hammer and nail (like a chisel) to split the plaster block at the layer made by the leaves to reveal the mold.

# Making a mold and cast of your teeth

## Procedure:

Press clay into lower portion of the cup. Press upper teeth into clay as deeply as possible (you are making a mold), being careful not to damage edge of cup. Rejoin edges of cup and tape over the incision. Use as much tape as necessary to completely seal the cut. After the halves of the cup are rejoined and taped, put the cup onto newspaper or on a tray before the next step, because if the tape seal is not tight, plaster will leak out of the cup. Pour plaster of paris into the cup (make it to a fairly fluid consistency, so air bubbles can be released more easily) and rap the base of cup several times on tabletop (this is to dislodge bubbles that may be trapped in the crevices). When the plaster has set (it should be good and hard), tear away cup and carefully peel clay away from the plaster to reveal a cast of your teeth.

## MATERIALS:

- ◆ paper cup
- ◆ tape (masking or duct tape, scotch tape is not as good)
- ◆ non-toxic modeling clay or plasticene
- ◆ sharp knife (Exacto knife or scalpel is good. Be careful!)
- ◆ plaster of paris
- ◆ plastic container for mixing plaster.

## FIGURE 1.1

Steps in making a cast of your teeth. Left: Cut paper cup, leaving a small section intact for a hinge. Middle: Fill with clay to the top of the cut and impress teeth. Right: Tape cup together tightly and add plaster.

# Simulating permineralization

MATERIALS:

- two bowls
- sand
- ordinary kitchen sponge
- salt
- warm water
- scissors
- spoon

After an organism is buried and its flesh has rotted away, only the skeleton or shell is left. Some of these hard parts, such as wood or bone, are porous, meaning they are filled with tiny holes. When water in the ground flows through these pores, the water leaves minerals that fill up the pores and turn the fossil into rock. This process is called permineralization and is the way petrified wood and much bone is preserved. One of the most common minerals to fill wood and bone in this way is silica. Cut and polished silicaized (agatized) wood and bone is very colorful and beautiful.

## Procedure:

Cut a piece of the sponge into a bone shape and bury it in sand in the bowl. Mix 2 parts salt to 5 parts warm water (e.g. 100 ml of salt to 250 ml of water) and pour the salt water into bowl (enough to completely soak the sand). Set bowl in a warm/sunny spot, under a hot lamp or in a low temperature oven (at around 250 degrees Fahrenheit, be sure to use a Pyrex bowl if you apply heat) and allow water to evaporate. In the oven, the block will dry in a few hours. If left out in the sun, it may take several days. Once dry, use the spoon to excavate your fossil. The sponge is hard because it soaked up the salty water and as the water dried, it left salt crystals in the pore spaces of the sponge. This is like permineralization: the manner in which most wood and bone is fossilized.

# Molecule-for-molecule replacement of fossils

Sometimes the chemical composition of a fossil changes due to conditions in the environment. For example, a bone that is buried in salty mud may have its open spaces fill with a particular salt. The bone will have been "permineralized." Original bone may remain around the spaces. At a later time the molecules that make up the original bone may be replaced by molecules of an entirely different and more stable substance. Fossilized wood or bone often forms in this way. The appearance—and even the microscopic structures of such tissues as bone and wood—is caused by molecule-for-molecule replacement. Many of the attractive shells of fossil mollusks are composed of replacement minerals much different from the original carbonate. A dramatic example of this phenomenon is the carbonate shells or ammonites that have been replaced by iron sulfide, or pyrite (fool's gold), giving the fossil the appearance of having been made of gold.

Fossilization by replacement can be demonstrated by a simple activity.

MATERIALS:

◆ lustrous steel wool (no coating)
◆ steel wire
◆ copper sulfate crystals

## Procedure:

Form the wire into the shape of a person about three inches high. Fill out the body with puffs of steel wool. Make a 2% solution of copper sulfate. Fill a container with copper sulfate solution so that you can immerse the little fellow up to its waist. In a few seconds the steel (iron) will begin being replaced by the copper in the solution and the iron will take the place of copper in the solution. In the end the copper fossil person is structurally identical to the original steel person.

### FIGURE 1.2

Wire figure used to simulate replacement.

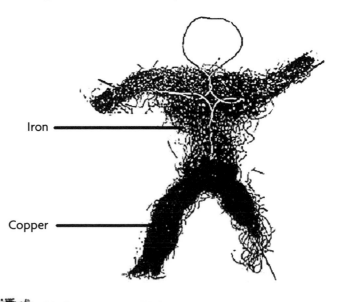

Iron

Copper

# Fossils in strata

## MATERIALS:

- sand
- plaster of paris
- container
- "fossil" material, such as sand, dirt, gravel, shells, etc.

SCI**LINKS**®
*THE WORLD'S A CLICK AWAY*

Topic: Sedimentary Rock
Go to: www.scilinks.org
Code: AP002

Fossils occur in sedimentary rock, which is rock that is composed of grains (such as sand or clay) that were laid down by water or wind. The mud or sand in a stream, lake, or desert may someday become deeply buried and turn into sedimentary rock. Sedimentary rock has layers or strata that reflect the natural rhythm of weather and deposition. For example, a stream flowing normally is usually clear because slowly moving water cannot move rocks or carry much sediment. But when the stream is flooding the water is higher and faster, and is brown because it is carrying more sand and clay. It is probably also carrying sticks and leaves and perhaps a dead animal. If the stream rises so much that it overflows its banks, it will deposit its load of sand, clay, sticks, and leaves in a layer on top of the stream banks. This layer of sand and debris is a sedimentary record of a flood event. Over time many such storms will leave a thick sequence of strata that records the history of the stream and its floods.

Different sedimentary environments have different types of deposits. For example, a beach deposit will typically consist of sand and seashells. A stream deposit may have sand, gravel, sticks, and leaves. A forest floor will have soil and plant debris.

When sediments are deposited, new layers are always laid on top of older ones. So in a stack of such layers, the youngest layer lies on top and the layers get progressively older as you go down.

You can make simulated sedimentary rock with fossils and have your own "dig" where you unearth and reconstruct past environments.

## Procedure:

Go to several different sedimentary environments and observe the conditions you find there and collect some sediment. You might go to a beach and collect some sand and shells and perhaps a small piece of driftwood or a bird feather. You might also collect material at a pond, a meadow, a lake, or a forest. Collect some sediment or soil from each and try to find some distinctive items that will identify the environment such as leaves, fish bones, seashells, and so on.

Figure out what geologic "story" you want to tell. For example one story might record what happens when sea level rises over a forest. This would involve a forest deposit overlain by a beach, overlain by deeper water sediments. As sea level falls, you might then expect to see another beach overlain by stream or forest deposits again. To make a sedimentary record of this sequence of events, first take a watertight container like a large plastic milk bottle or cardboard milk carton. Cut off the top and then put in layers of sediment that represent the different environments you want to portray. To portray the sea level rise and fall mentioned above, start by placing a layer of the "oldest" environment (forest soil) at the bottom of the carton. Place over this a layer of beach deposits and some broken shell (as you might find on a beach), followed by some finer sediment and more shells to represent the deeper water of the sea. The sea level fall would be the reverse of this, i.e., laying another beach layer over the deep water sediment and that in turn would be overlain by more forest or maybe a stream deposit. Try to place as many "fossils" and other interesting artifacts (feathers, fish or chicken bones, bottle caps, coins) in the mix as you can. You could even add a layer of modeling clay that had "tracks" in it. Once you have placed all the layers in the container, you can turn this sedimentary sequence into "rock" by making a dilute mixture of plaster of paris and water (about 3 tablespoons of plaster to 1/2 cup of water) and adding it to the sediment in the container. Slowly pour the liquid into the container until the whole thing is saturated. Let the block dry completely; at least one to two days, depending on the size of the container. Once dry you can cut or peel away the container and see the layers from the side exactly the way they would look if you were at a real rock outcrop. The dried mixture should be firm enough to be rock-like but soft enough to easily dig with a spoon or butter knife. In the classroom students should each have a brush and a digging tool. As they work from the top of the block down, they should describe the sediment, retrieve the "fossils" and identify and label them and place them in small containers just like a real paleontologist. An entry in their notes might look like this:

Layer 1—Sand and gravel with leaves and a small bone. Probably a stream deposit.
Layer 2—Fine sand with whole and broken seashells. Possibly a beach deposit, etc.

Once they have excavated the entire block, they can reconstruct the sequence of events that took place. Remember the actual sequence is the REVERSE of the order in which they were excavated. In other words, the last or most recent event that happened is represented by the top or first layer that was excavated and the first or oldest event is at the bottom of the block.

## FIGURE 1.3

Making simulated fossils in strata. Left: Fill cardboard or plastic carton with layers of sediment and "fossil" objects. Middle: Add dilute plaster mixture until thoroughly soaked. Right: After it dries, peel away sides of container and excavate.

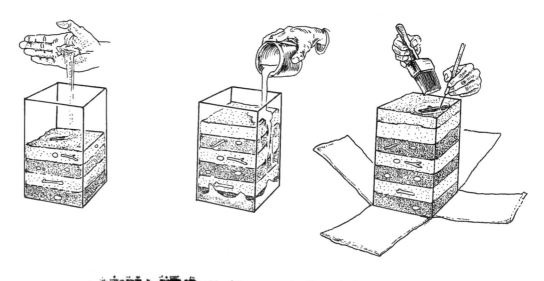

# Inventing ways to make fossils of grapes and bananas

## MATERIALS:

- ◆ fresh grapes
- ◆ banana
- ◆ shrimp
- ◆ fish
- ◆ cubic foot of forest floor litter and soil.

Plants, animals, and microorganisms have life cycles. They come into being, live for a while, and then die. There are no known exceptions. In this activity you will investigate what can happen to the remains of organisms when they die. In the second part of the activity, you will investigate alternative ways you can preserve a dead organism so that evidence of its existence will last indefinitely. Objectives of this activity are to 1) observe and record the physical and chemical changes in the body of a dead organism over a period of time, 2) explore and describe the dead organism in a cubic foot of litter and soil from a forest floor, and 3) devise ways to preserve evidence of the existence of your dead organism.

## Procedure:

- ◆ Obtain about a dozen fresh grapes and/or a banana. Imagine that these fleshy fruits represent even larger fleshy dead organisms.
- ◆ Place one grape and/or one slice of banana in an open dish. Observe what happens to these "dead organisms" over a period of several months.
- ◆ Place a cubic foot of forest floor litter and soil on a large sheet of butcher paper. Beginning at the top of the cube, carefully remove each layer of material. The top layer should be the most recent accumulation of leaves, twigs, lichens from the over-hanging trees. As you go deeper into the cube you should encounter increasingly older plant material. Using pictures describe the fate of plant materials that fall onto the forest floor.
- ◆ Select other grapes or pieces of bananas. How many different ways can you preserve the fruit so that your descendants one million years from this day will have at hand evidence of the existence of your grape or banana slice? In a sense you will manufacture a fossil.

## Analysis:

- ◆ What was the fate of exposed grapes and banana slices?
- ◆ What appears to be the fate of dead materials that accumulate on a forest floor?
- ◆ List the ways you, and others, were able to produce fruit fossils from fresh grapes and banana slices.
- ◆ Fossils you made from fresh fruit are artificial in the sense that the preservation was manmade and not the way fossils form in nature. Under what circumstances do you think fossil grapes and bananas might form in nature?

## Going Further:

For various reasons, most human cultures do not allow dead bodies to lie around and decompose. A large human industry manages the disposal of dead people, pets, or other organisms. Which methods of disposal of bodies recycle them? Which methods tend to preserve bodies and thus create artificial fossils?

# Fossils in amber

Interest in amber has soared since the book and movie, *Jurassic Park*, captured the imagination of the public. In the story scientists found Jurassic Period mosquitoes in amber that had sucked the blood of dinosaurs. By collecting the blood of the dinosaurs and amplifying the DNA in the white blood cells, the scientists were able to produce the animals from which the blood was taken. As a result, the scientists populated an entire island with extinct animals. Real life later copied fiction when scientists extracted DNA from insects in amber from ancient ages. Dr. Raúl Cano of California Polytechnic State University and colleagues reported having extracted and sequenced DNA from a weevil embedded in amber from the age of dinosaurs (1993). Dr. Cano also caused excitement when he reported having cultured live symbiotic bacteria from the abdomens of stingless bees preserved in 40 million year old amber from the Dominican Republic (1994).

In this activity you will polish a piece of rough amber to a clarity that will enable you to see fossil inclusions. Only rarely will you find a flower or an insect in amber. However, it is rare to find a piece of amber that does not contain *some* trace of past life.

## MATERIALS:

- ◆ specimen of rough amber
- ◆ 80-, 280-, and 600-grit sandpaper
- ◆ cerium oxide polish
- ◆ denim cloth for polishing
- ◆ dissecting and compound microscopes
- ◆ magnifying glass.

## Procedure:

Begin using 80-grit sandpaper if the rough amber is jagged and coarse. Wear the amber ore down to expose the yellow-orange amber on all sides. Use 280-grit sandpaper to expose at least two surfaces of your amber. Round off the sharp edges of your piece. Use 600-grit sandpaper to polish the specimen to a shine. Dampen the swatch of denim cloth with water, and lightly sprinkle the amber with cerium oxide, or other jeweler's polish. You can use toothpaste in place of cerium oxide. Polish the sanded piece of amber until the clear faces of the specimen are free of scratches.

Examine the polished piece of amber with a dissecting microscope, or thin slices with a compound microscope. Use 10x or 20x hand lenses for spot checks. When you find an interesting inclusion, record sketches of it, from several angles, on drawing paper. The organisms of the Cenozoic Era (about 65 million years ago to the present) are not so different from the insect and plants of today that you can't identify them to family and often to genus.

If you have a piece of rough copal—a specimen much younger in age than amber—you should proceed to polish it in the same manner as the amber. The finished product can be used for science study, or for a pretty gift for a loved one.

## What is amber?

Amber is fossil resin secreted by tropical flowering and conifer trees in response to wounds inflicted by boring insects, mechanical injuries, or just growth. Resins apparently provide a mechanism for sealing bark wounds and inhibiting an attack by insects and herbivores.

## FIGURE 1.4

Insect being trapped in tree sap that will eventually become amber.
Drawn by Hazen Audel.

Resin also inhibits the growth of bacteria and fungi. Unlike gums, resins are not water soluble. Under conditions of moderate temperature, pressure, absence of air, and probably submergence in seawater, resins can remain intact in sediment for hundreds of millions years.

Chemically, amber is a mixture of terpenoids that make up the resin and which forms after approximately 4 to 5 million years of polymerization and oxidation. Before becoming amber, the resin is in a form called **copal**. Resins become copal as soon as the resins lose their pliability. Fresh resin and copal from tropical rain forest are used today as a source of varnish. In the nineteenth century tons of Baltic amber were melted down for varnish.

Resins should not be confused with sap, which is the water solution transported through the xylem and phloem (as maple syrup), or with gums, which are polysaccharides produced in plants as a result of bacterial infections. Ten percent of plant families produce resins, and most are tropical flowering plants. All conifers produce resins, but only pines and araucarians produce large quantities. The amber of the Dominican Republic and Mexico were produced by trees of the legume family of the genus *Hymenaea*. One of the major suppliers of modern resins in the tropics is a related species of *Hymenaea*.

Amber of the temperate Baltic coast originated about 50 million years ago from the resins from the conifera family Araucariaceae. Evidence suggests that pine, once thought to be the major source of fossil resin, does not fossilize into amber. Since the infrared absorption spectrum of the conifer of Araucariaceae genus *Agathis* is dramatically similar to the spectrum of Baltic amber, many paleontologists think that *Agathis*, and not *Pinus*, represents the ancestral source of Baltic amber. Today, *Hymenaea* is distributed in South and Central America and Africa, and *Agathis* is distributed in parts of Asia, Europe, North America, and the West Indies. The dawn redwood *Metasequoia glyptostroboides* is a descendant of the ancient trees that produced amber in the Pacific Northwest about 50 million years ago.

The process of amberization apparently requires that the polymerization of monomers (isoprenes) in fresh amber proceeds in decay-resistant environments, protected from the elements, inundated for a time by sea water, and never exposed the temperatures over 80 degrees Celsius or high tectonic pressures.

## Inclusions in Amber

Fresh amber on the trunk of a tree works like fly paper. As the organism sinks in, and as the resin continues to flow, the things that stick onto the resin become embedded before the glob of resin falls off the tree, or the tree rots away leaving just the resin (Figure 1.4).

Inclusions reveal the diversity of forest life. In the 25- to 40-million-years-old amber found in the Dominican Republic, the resin entombed insects, spiders, frogs, feathers, leopard fur, flowers, bacteria, molds, mosses, rotifers, snails, leaves, buds, and a zillion unidentified pieces of debris including bubbles, now filled with gas and/or liquid. While the organisms died in the soft resin, standing waves from the frantic movement of an appendage can sometimes be seen in the amber. After death, internal parasites such as worms, or external parasites such as mites, can be seen leaving the host. Mold, often with fruiting bodies and spores, can be seen on the organic debris. But the resins are powerful antibiotics and decomposition of organic material is minimal.

Some animals like long-legged spiders may leave a leg or two in the resin. A bird or a mammal brushing against the resin may leave a feather or a tuft of hair behind. As mammals trapped in the La Brea tars of California, or the dinosaurs in the mud of Tendaguru in East Africa, so too were the entrapped organisms in resins eaten away by predators and scavengers.

Most Dominican Republic amber is clear and golden in color, allowing biological inclusions to be seen. In contrast, Baltic amber is often cloudy due to the large numbers of air bubbles in the resin. Popular colors of cloudy amber range from a milky golden to a chalky white depending on the size and the number of bubbles. Since amber melts readily (200–360 degrees Celsius), it absorbs color and oils, and accepts new inclusions easily. Altered amber can be made to appear more attractive than natural amber.

Cano, R. J. 1994. Ancient bacillus DNA: A window to ancient symbiotic relationships? *ASM News.* 60(3): 129–134.

Cano, R. J., H. N. Poinar, N. S. Pieniazek, and G. O. Poinar Jr. 1993. Enzymatic amplification and nucleotide sequencing of DNA from 120–135 million year old weevil. *Nature* 363: 536–538.

# What Can You Learn From Fossils?

## Scientific Inquiry

What is scientific inquiry and how does it work? Scientific inquiry refers to the processes that help us to understand how the natural world works. (Note: This is different from the scientific method. The term *scientific method* is misleading, as there is no one "set-in-stone" approach to scientific research. Instead, scientists use a variety of approaches in their research, and are able to alter steps and go in new directions as the research demands. For example, penicillin, x-rays, and vulcanized rubber were all "accidental" discoveries, brought about because scientists altered the course of the research in response to unexpected findings.) There is nothing mysterious about scientific inquiry and we all use it everyday. It starts with facts that are objectively observable or measurable. We obtain these facts by observations of a natural phenomenon such as, "My car won't start." This initial factual observation might be followed by more information, like, "When I turn the key, nothing happens." Based on these facts you form a hypothesis to explain why your car won't start such as: "My battery is dead." This hypothesis allows you to make some predictions such as: "If the battery is dead, my dome light will not work or will be dim. Also, my headlights won't work or will be dim." You can then test the hypothesis by checking your predictions; look at your dome lights and your headlights. If these lights all work fine, then it suggests the battery is not the problem. You could further test the dead battery hypothesis by replacing the battery with one that you know is good. If the car still does not start, then clearly the dead battery hypothesis has failed (or been falsified) and a new hypothesis must be formulated, e.g., "The starter motor is bad." It is important to note here that all scientific hypotheses are tentative and must be discarded if they fail critical tests. In this case, it would be foolish to keep replacing the battery with new ones in the belief that the dead battery hypothesis *must* be right. It is also important to note that the hypotheses above invoke natural causes and are all testable. It would not be scientific to suggest a supernatural hypothesis such as: "My car is cursed" because this would not be testable. You cannot see or measure a curse and you cannot remove it to see if your car then functions properly. This is not to say that your car is not cursed, it is just that the statement "My car is cursed" is not scientific because it invokes a supernatural phenomenon that cannot be tested.

Scientists propose hypotheses to explain many natural phenomena, such as why mountains form or why the Moon orbits Earth. When these hypotheses survive repeated tests by many scientists, they may be elevated to the status of scientific theory (e.g., Theory of Relativity, Theory of Evolution). Therefore a scientific theory is not just a guess or an opinion, it is a well-established scientific explanation for natural phenomena that has been tested many times and not falsified. A scientific law represents an even higher level of certainty. A scientific law is a statement of fact generally accepted to be true and universal

SCI LINKS
THE WORLD'S A CLICK AWAY

Topic: Scientific Inquiry
Go to: www.scilinks.org
Code: AP003

because they have always been observed to be true (e.g., the Law of Gravity, the Law of Thermodynamics).

You can practice scientific inquiry with your class with a variety of props. For example bring in a table lamp and place it on a desk. You should "disable" the lamp by putting in a bad bulb or loosening the bulb and leaving it unplugged. Turn the lamp switch and asked the students to make observations, e.g., "the lamp does not work." Now have them propose hypotheses for why the lamp does not work. For example:

◆ Hypothesis 1: The lamp is not plugged in.
◆ Hypothesis 2: The bulb is bad.
◆ Hypothesis 3: The bulb is not screwed in.
◆ Hypothesis 4: The electricity is not working.

Now test each hypothesis by plugging the lamp in, screwing in the bulb, testing the bulb in another lamp, etc., until the correct hypothesis is found. The main points to be made here are that:

1. Scientific inquiry is not mysterious or intimidating, we all use it everyday.
2. Scientific inquiry deals only with observable natural phenomena and does not invoke supernatural causes.
3. Scientific inquiry is a series of processes and its conclusions are tentative. We must be willing to alter our hypotheses to accommodate new evidence.

## TEACHER'S NOTES:

The purpose of this set of activities is to enable student to engage in the same kind of investigative study as do paleontologists. Activities 1–3 progress from reconstructing an entire living human using evidence gathered from an examination of only that person's hand, to the reconstruction and restoration of an authentic 150 million-year-old pterosaur fossil.

### Reconstructing *Scaphognathus crassirostris* and Restoring
*Scaphognathus crassirostris*
Important in the conduct of these activities is for the student to recognize that the reconstruction and restoration of the mystery fossil is authentic. They are solving the problem Georg August Goldfuss confronted in the 1820s. Goldfuss used the original fossil on a slab of limestone (Figure 2.3) to draw the bones in the skeleton (Figure 2.5). Two Goldfuss errors should noted: (1) Goldfuss miscounted the number of fingers with claws. There should be three on each forearm. We corrected this error. (2) This was the first specimen of *Scaphognathus crassirostris* discovered. It had no tail; and Goldfuss drew it without a tail. Later a specimen from the same limestone formation was found with a fully intact long tail.

An assembled skeleton of Goldfuss's *Scaphognathus crassirostris* appears in Figure 2.6 as students might assemble the bones. Few students can fully assemble the bones without help. The real or drawn skeletons of bats and birds and other vertebrates will help students figure out the sequence of appendage bone and vertebrae. Getting the giant finger in position often requires an intuitive leap.

Restoring the living fossil and placing it in a suitable environment challenges the serious student to be scientifically accurate and imaginative at the same time. Figure 2.7 includes a sample of professional restoration of *Scaphognathus crassirostris*.

## FIGURE 2.6

Reconstructed skeleton of *Scaphognathus crassirostris*.

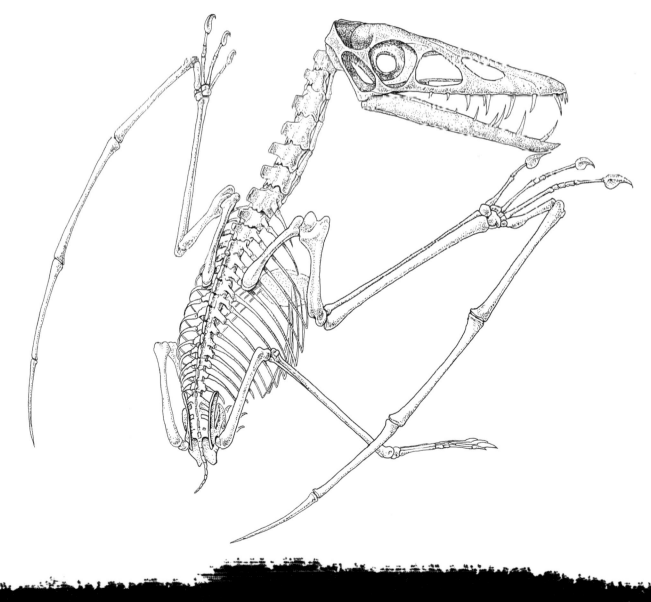

FIGURE 2.7

Life restoration of *Scaphognathus crassirostris*.

**Question: What was the purpose of the plates on the back of *Stegosaurus*?** .................... CHAPTER 2, ACTIVITY 9

This is a guided discussion activity that practices using scientific inquiry on a question about *Stegosaurus*. You might start by asking the question and then letting the students come up with as many different hypotheses as they can about the purpose of the plates. Then help them clarify what they mean about each hypothesis. For example if a student says the plates were for "defense," you should ask them to give an example of a living animal that does this which will then allow you to make predictions to test these hypotheses. This activity is an example of how this discussion might proceed.

# Inferring the characteristics of people from their hands

MATERIALS:

- mystery person
- dark cloth to cover a doorway with small slit for hand
- chair
- desk
- ruler
- magnifying glass
- clock with second hand

What can you tell about people by examining only their hands? How close could you estimate the person's age? What clues would you look for in the appearance and texture of the skin, the condition of the fingernails, the feel of finger bones and joints, the behavior of the hand of the hidden person? What other characteristics of the person can you infer from the hand?

This activity is a model of how paleontologists construct stories about fossils they find and study. In the model the hand is the fossil and the person behind the screen is the unknown organism from the past. Ordinarily, paleontologists know about as much about fossils and the whole extinct organism as you know about hands and people. The more you study the hands of people, the better you become in predicting what people are like by examining their hands.

## Objectives:

1. Observe, measure, and record characteristics of one hand of a person sitting outside your view.
2. Infer the characteristics of the whole mystery person and draw a composite picture.

## Procedures:

1. Make a list of characteristics you can infer by examining the hands of people (Figure 2.1). Next to each characteristic describe the clues you will look for in the hand to give good ideas about the whole person. Perhaps you will do this planning the day before the hand of the mystery person enters your classroom through a hole in the sheet that covers the doorway.
2. After the hand appears at the doorway, examine the hand with your group. On the table with the hand should be some instruments for examining features of the hand: a magnifying glass to see the color of hair, a ruler to compare the finger lengths of the mystery hand and your own, and a clock with a second hand to compare the pulse of the hand with your own. Record your data. After returning to your seat, study your data. Then write a description of the mystery person, including its physical appearance, its behaviors and anything else you can infer.
3. After the class has discussed everyone's observations and inferences, a class composite of the mystery person can be assembled. Since the mystery person represents a whole living fossil, something paleontologists never get to see, perhaps the activity would be more true to science if the class would never see the mystery person. The class will have to decide whether the mystery person (fossil) should ever show itself.

Topic: Population Characteristics
Go to: www.scilinks.org
Code: AP004

FIGURE 2.1

Students attempting to discern characteristics of a mystery person by his hand.

## Going Further:

What can you infer about a nation by studying just the coins or stamps the government issued? What can archeologists tell about an ancient civilization by examining buried trash piles? What can police scientists infer from hair, blood, or auto tracks found at a crime scene?

Examine the picture of the skeleton below. What can you infer about the biology of this animal from what you observe here?

## FIGURE 2.2

Skeleton of a bat.

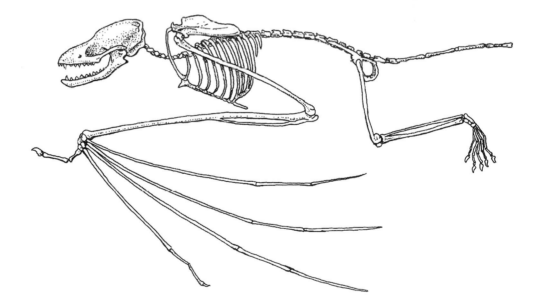

# Reconstructing
# *Scaphognathus crassirostris*

MATERIALS:

◆ scissors
◆ ruler
◆ transparent tape
◆ photocopy of exact-size fossil bones

The fossilized remains of the animal illustrated in Figure 2.3 were found in a limestone quarry in Germany in 1826. About one hundred and fifty million years ago, the quarry was a deep ocean lagoon (Figure 2.4). Organisms that died and sank to the bottom of the lagoon were buried by fine particles of lime mud. Fine details of organisms were preserved in the limestone. Water currents did not redistribute skeletons.

Georg August Goldfuss was the scientist who found the specimen. He cut out a slab of limestone with the fossil and took it to his laboratory for study. Goldfuss reconstructed the bones of the fossil animal, and then put the bones together to form a complete skeleton in a lifelike posture.

The purpose of this activity is for you to try to solve the very same mystery Goldfuss confronted. What did the assembled skeleton of this fossil animal look like? And then: What kind of life did this animal live in Germany about 150 million years ago?

FIGURE 2.3

Original specimen of *Scaphognathus crassirostris* found by Goldfuss.

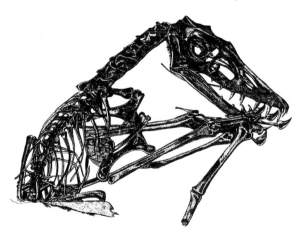

FIGURE 2.4

Reconstruction of lagoon environment in which *Scaphognathus crassirostris* was deposited.

## Objectives:

1. Reconstruct the skeleton of a mystery fossil from the Jurassic Period.
2. Make inferences about what the fossil animal looked like when alive, what food it ate, and its mode of transportation.

## Procedure:

1. Cut out the life-size pictures of the mystery fossil's bones as originally drawn by Goldfuss (Figure 2.5).
2. Use your knowledge about vertebrate skeletons and if available, the pictures of skeletons of such familiar animals as mammals, birds, and lizards. Begin your assembly at the head with the skull and jaw. Lay out the bones of the neck, chest, hip, and tail. Add the smaller leg bones to the hip. The thigh bone fits into the hip bone. A single leg bone connects with the thigh (you have two leg bones in each of your own legs). The small 4-toe feet connect with the leg bones. The larger upper arm bones connect with the shoulder blades. The lower arm bones are composed of two fused bones, to which the hand connects at the wrist. The fifth finger of each hand of the fossil is almost as large as its entire body.

When your skeleton is assembled to your satisfaction, fix it in position by taping the bones together. You may wish to mount the model skeleton on a piece of poster paper.

## Analysis:

1. How tall was the animal? _____ How wide was the animal when spread out? ___ _____ Most animals barely float in water. Knowing the approximate volume of the animal and the density of water, what do you estimate the weight of the animal to be? _____
2. What do you think was the function of the huge finger on each hand?
3. What modern animals do you think this fossil was most like? In what ways does it appear to have differed from modern animals that may live like it did?
4. What do the teeth in the skull and jaw tell you about feeding habits? How do you explain the large open spaces in the skull, the hollow long bones? The small feet with tiny claws and the large hands with large claws?

FIGURE 2.5

Life-size picture of the fossil as originally drawn by Goldfuss.

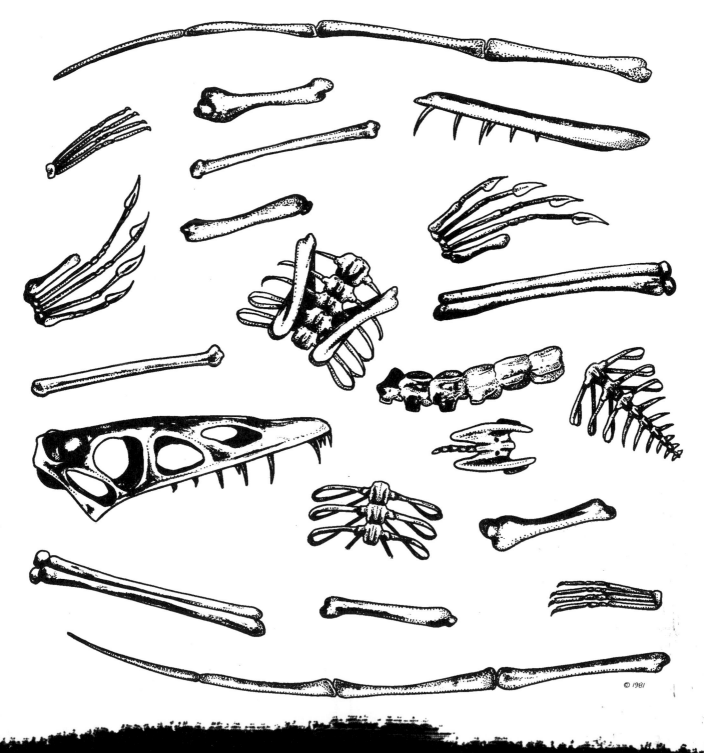

© 1981

# Restoring
# *Scaphognathus crassirostris*

MATERIALS:

- crayons
- water paints
- poster paper
- clay

Once paleontologists have reconstructed the skeleton of a fossil vertebrate (Figure 2.6), they begin thinking about the appearance of the living animal, its habitat, how it lived with other organisms, and how it was adapted to its physical environment. In this part of the activity you have the opportunity to restore the fossil and put it into the environment to which it was adapted. For an example of the product of this approach see Figure 2.7.

## Procedure:

1. Look at the fossil skeleton for several minutes. Think about who this animal was, living around 150 million years ago in a tropical land by the sea now known as Germany. Measure the length of the head and the length of the body. Imagine how it might have moved about: For what purposes did it use the claws on its fingers? Was its skin bare, or was there a protective and/or insulating covering?
2. Now in the imaginative part of your mind pretend you and this beautiful beast are buddies. Spend a Jurassic day together: Travel together, eat together, double date. Become part of its life. Call it by its scientific name, *Scaphognathus crassirostris*.
3. Draw and color a scientifically accurate portrait of *Scaphognathus crassirostris* in a typical pose. Include in the background of the portrait evidence of its modes of locomotion, feeding behavior, and its habitat. You may wish to create a sculpture of the animal and include elements of its environment. See Figure 2.6 for an example of a reconstruction.
4. On the reverse of the picture, or on separate paper, make a list of questions about *Scaphognathus crassirostris*—questions you truly wish to answer.

## Going Further:

According to the latest counts, 20 families, 40 genera, and 100 species of pterosaurs have been discovered and described from the Triassic, Jurassic, and Cretaceous Periods. *Scaphognathus* was one of the 40 genera that included two species, *Scaphognathus crassirostris* and *Scaphognathus purdoni*. Pterosaurs ranged in size from the sparrow-like *Anurognathus* to the small airplane-sized *Quetzalcoatlus*. Pterosaurs lived for about 120 million years and were the dominant airborne vertebrates of the Mesozoic Era. Pterosaurs lived and died out with the dinosaurs. What can you find out about the evolution of pterosaurs? How did they relate with birds? How could the birds have survived the mass extinction crisis of 65 million years ago, but not the pterosaurs? What factors do you think contributed to pterosaur extinction?

ACTIVITY 4

# Tracking dinosaurs

Tracks and traces are unique as fossils because they provide direct evidence of *behavior* in extinct animals. For instance, tracks can tell us if dinosaurs walked with their legs spread wide apart like a crocodile or closer together like a horse. Tracks can tell us how fast animals ran, or whether they traveled in herds. There is even a trackway that suggests a dinosaur stampede!

Let's see how much we can tell from the dinosaur trackways at left (Figure 2.8):

First, we can see that there are two trackways made by two different kinds of dinosaurs. We can also tell that both dinosaurs walked on two legs (bipeds) because the tracks are evenly spaced apart. The tracks of four legged animals (quadrupeds) tend to occur in pairs. You can demonstrate this by walking on a sheet of butcher paper with wet socks.

**FIGURE 2.8**

Trackway of a carnosaur and a hadrosaur.

**FIGURE 2.9**

Human tracks made on paper. Top: walking normally. Bottom: walking on all fours.

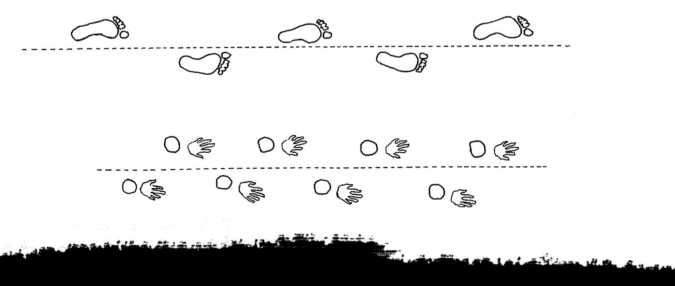

## FIGURE 2.10

Tracks made by a hadrosaur, allosaur, ankylosaur, and sauropod.

First walk normally and see how the footprints are evenly spaced and occur along a line. Then walk on all fours and notice how the prints are paired and also spread apart laterally. You could get really fancy and make a tail to drag along, producing a tail-drag mark. Note that sauropod dinosaur trackways almost never show a tail-drag mark. What does this tell us about how sauropods held their tails?

Use the Dinosaur Track Field Guide at right (Figure 2.10) to identify the dinosaurs that made the trackways on the previous page.

**Hadrosaur**    **Allosaur**    **Ankylosaur**    **Sauropod**

## FIGURE 2.11

Outline of a *Tyrannosaurus rex* footprint.

It is also possible to guess the size of the dinosaur that made a track. Generally the length of a dinosaur footprint was 1/4 the length of the leg (1/5 in the case of some of the skinnier bipeds such as the coelurosaurs). Since most dinosaurs walked with their backbones parallel to the ground, this is also a rough measure of their "height." The largest *Tyrannosaurus rex* (tyrannosaur) footprint ever found was 34 inches in length. Make an overhead transparency of the footprint (Figure 2.11) and project it at actual size (34 inches long) to get a feel for just how big this is. What was the leg length of the dinosaur that made this print?

How long was the tyrannosaur that made the track in Figure 2.11? This can be determined by comparing the leg length with the length of the body in Figure 2.12 below. The leg length is what fraction of the overall length? How long was the tyrannosaur that made the track?

## FIGURE 2.12

Skeleton of an adult *Tyrannosaurus rex*.

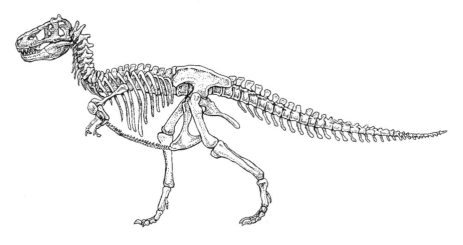

Now try another demonstration with the butcher paper. First walk normally and then speed up. Notice how the footprints get farther apart with increased speed (Figure 2.13).

Now how would you interpret the trackway below? What dinosaur made the tracks and what did it do?

Putting everything we have learned together, how would you interpret the trackway below (Figure 2.15)? What dinosaurs made the tracks, how big were they, what happened?

## FIGURE 2.13

Human footprints. Top: spacing seen in a slow walk. Bottom: spacing seen in a fast walk.

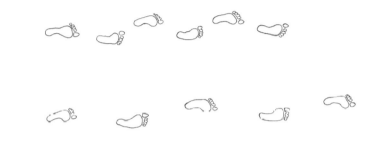

## FIGURE 2.14

Hadrosaur tracks indicating a change of direction and an increase in speed.

## FIGURE 2.15

Hadrosaur tracks indicating change of direction and speed. Carnosaur tracks on intercept course and speeding up.

Duckbill dinosaurs (ornithopods) are one of the few dinosaur groups where it is not obvious how they walked, i.e., on two or four legs. Their forelegs were large enough to reach the ground comfortably, so they could have walked on all four legs (quadrupedal, Figure 2.16) or on two legs (bipedal, Figure 2.17).

Figure 2.18 is the track of a kind of ornithopod called a hadrosaur. What does this track tell us about how hadrosaurs walked?

How would you interpret the trackway in Figure 2.19?

With these tools, you can make additional scenarios, or have the students make their own. You can use the templates provided in the following figures to make your own tracks and lay them out across the floor. With their Dinosaur Track Field Guides and rulers, the students can identify the dinosaurs, calculate their sizes, and reconstruct their behavior.

## FIGURE 2.16

Hadrosaur walking quadrupedally.

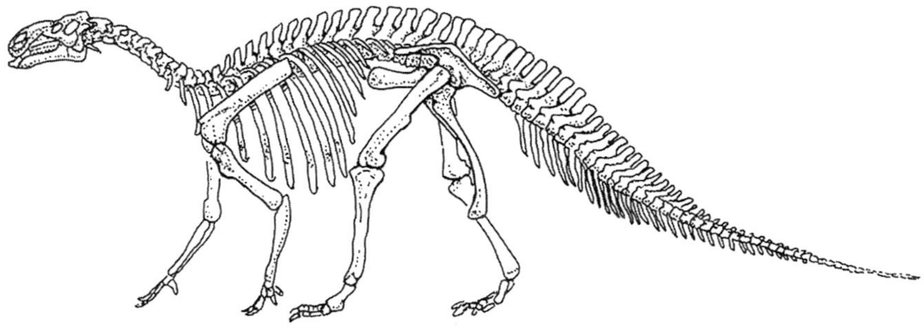

## FIGURE 2.17

Hadrosaur walking bipedally.

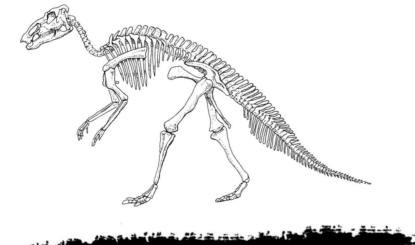

## FIGURE 2.18

Trackway of a hadrosaur.

## FIGURE 2.19

Trackways of three sauropods; two adults and one juvenile.

### FIGURE 2.20

Footprint of a hadrosaur.

### FIGURE 2.21

Left front (left) and left rear (right) footprints of the sauropod dinosaur *Diplodocus.*

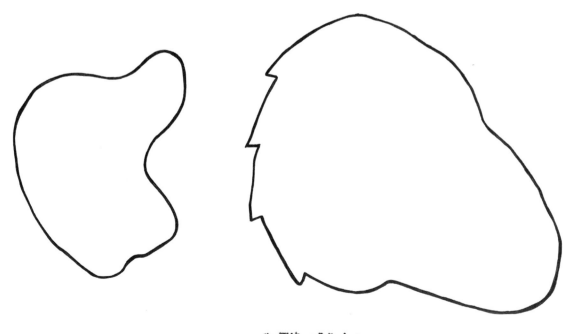

# Weighing dinosaurs

MATERIALS:

◆ watertight container
◆ pan to catch overflow
  of water
◆ dinosaur model

*Tyrannosaurus* may have weighed 7 tons. *Brachiosaurus* perhaps weighed 55 tons. Where do these figures come from? How can scientists calculate the weight of an extinct animal? One way is to just take a scale model of a dinosaur, measure the weight of the water it displaces and scale up for the dinosaur weight. Here's the reasoning. All animals are about the same density as water. We are mostly composed of water, and the weight of the heavier parts like bone is offset by the air spaces in our lungs. You can test this by getting in a pool. If you take a deep breath and lie face down in the water, you will float. Most people will tend to sink when they exhale. Therefore we (and most other animals) have a density near that of water [a density of 1.0]. So it stands to reason if you take an accurate scale model of a dinosaur, measure the weight of the water it displaces and then scale this number up, you will get a reasonable estimate of the weight of the dinosaur. The tricky part is that a scale, say 1/10 scale, is a *linear* scale. It only measures one dimension, while a dinosaur is a 3-dimensional object. Therefore when you scale up the weight of your model, say 5 fluid ounces, you must multiply this number by 40 x 40 x 40, or 40 cubed, to get the approximate weight of the dinosaur. Of course the accuracy of your estimate is very dependent on the accuracy of the scale model. For example, if the reconstruction of the dinosaur in the model is too skinny, then the final weight estimate can be very far off.

## Procedure:

1. Place the watertight container inside of pan and fill the container with water to the very brim.
2. Now carefully place the dinosaur model into container, allowing the water to spill out into the pan. You should use a good quality scale model such as those produced by the British Museum or the Carnegie Institute if you want an accurate estimate. But any model will work.
3. Now carefully remove the container without spilling any additional water and measure the amount of water in the pan. This is the displacement of your model. You can use a standard measuring cup or one graduated in milliliters. A fluid ounce of water weighs close to one ounce (remember, a pint is a pound the whole world around) and a milliliter of waters weighs one gram.

FIGURE 2.22

Apparatus used to measure the volume of a dinosaur model.

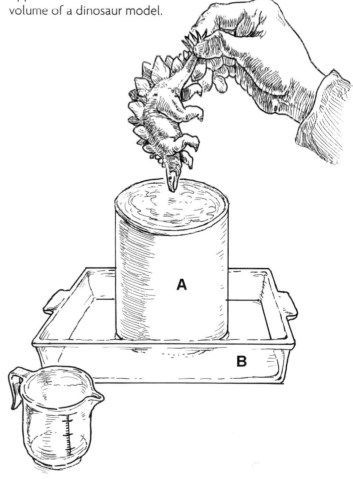

Topic: Using Models
Go to: www.scilinks.org
Code: AP005

Now follow these calculations:

|  | Standard | Metric |
|---|---|---|
| Displacement of model: | 5 fluid oz. | 148 milliliters |
| Weight of model: | 5 ounces (approx.) | 148 grams |
| Scale of model: | 1/40 | 1/40 |
| Weight scale cubed: | 5 x 40³ = 320,000 oz | 148 x 40³ = 9,472,000 gm |
| Est. dinosaur weight: | 320,000 oz or 20,000 lbs. | 9,472,000 gm or 9,472 kg |

## How to determine the scale of your model

Good scale models will usually tell you the scale; the Carnegie and British Museum models are 1/40 scale. But if you don't know the scale, or if you want to measure your own models, the scale is simple to determine. Measure the length of your model (*lm*) and divide that into the length of the dinosaur (*ld*).

Length of model (*lm*) = 8 inches
Length of dinosaur (*ld*) = 100 feet or 1,200 inches
*ld/lm* = 150 or 1/150 scale

## Going Further:

Commercial models such as those by the Carnegie Institute, are made for normal adult dinosaurs at a 1/40 scale. So measuring the displacement of the *Brachiosaurus* model and scaling up by 40 cubed will give you the weight of a normal adult *Brachiosaurus*. It can be fun to estimate the weight of the largest dinosaurs such as *Ultrasauros*, *Supersaurus*, or *Seismosaurus* (or for other animals, such as whales) by changing the scale and using the appropriate model. An *Ultrasauros* is simply a huge dinosaur very much like a *Brachiosaurus* (*Seismosaurus* and *Supersaurus* were shaped much like *Diplodocus* or *Apatosaurus*). To estimate the weight of *Supersaurus*, take a *Diplodocus* model and divide its length (lm, about 1.5 feet) into the length of *Supersaurus* (ld, around 140 feet).

*ld/lm* = 140 feet/1.5 feet = 93.3333 or a scale of about 1/93
Then follow the same procedure that you would for any other model.

# Learning the bones

In this exercise you will need to learn the bones of the arms and legs. All vertebrate animals that live on land have the same basic arrangement of bones in their limbs.

They have a single large bone in the upper arm (humerus) or upper leg (femur), two long bones in the lower arm (radius and ulna) or lower leg (tibia and fibula), small bones in the wrist (carpals) and ankle (tarsals), bones in the palm of the hand (metacarpals) and foot (metatarsals), and fingers and toes (digits).

## How was a dinosaur different from other reptiles?

Living reptiles have a sprawling or semi-sprawling posture meaning that their legs are held out to the sides of their bodies. Dinosaurs, mammals, and birds hold their legs directly beneath their bodies in an erect stance. Because mammals, birds, and dinosaurs use their legs in the same way, we can look at the bones of living animals, whose relative speeds we know, to help determine the running speeds of dinosaurs.

## FIGURE 2.23

Human (left) and crocodile (right) leg.

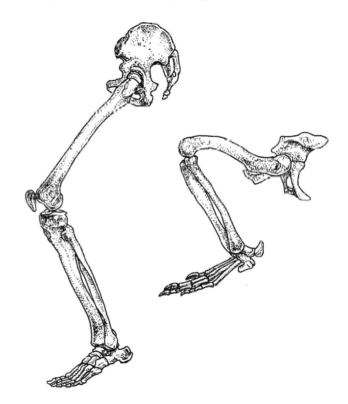

## FIGURE 2.24

Postures of a sprawling, semi-erect, and erect animals.

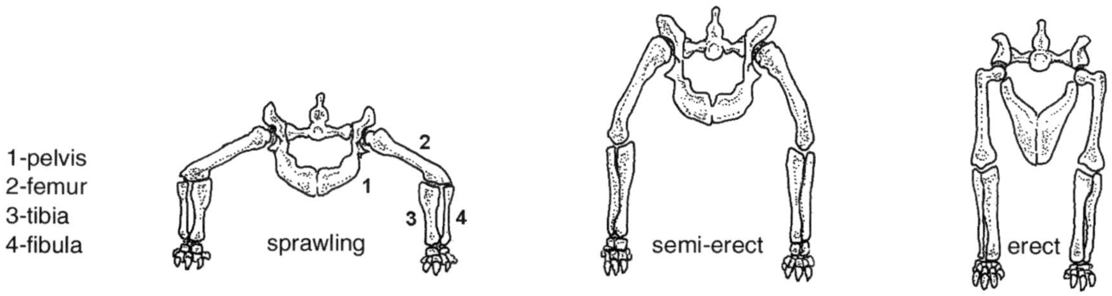

1-pelvis
2-femur
3-tibia
4-fibula

sprawling          semi-erect          erect

## FIGURE 2.25

Hind limbs of an armadillo (left), coyote (middle), and antelope (right).

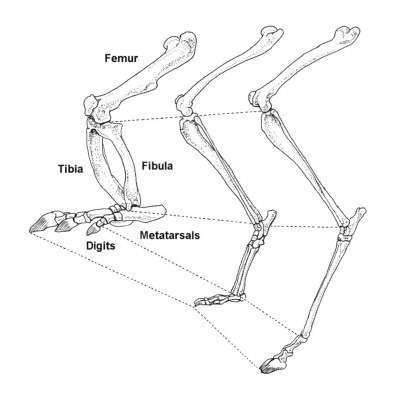

Femur

Tibia

Fibula

Digits

Metatarsals

Figure 2.25 shows the hind legs of three different mammals (an armadillo, coyote, and antelope) arranged according to speed and drawn so that the femur lengths are the same. The armadillo is the slowest and the antelope is the fastest. What observations can you make about how the legs differ as the animal gets faster?

Based on your observations from the armadillo, coyote, and antelope legs, how fast do you think the animals in Figure 2.26 are? Which is fastest, slowest, and in between?

Now let's see if you are correct. Figure 2.27 shows how these animals would perform in a race.

Now assess the speeds of the dinosaurs in Figure 2.28.

## FIGURE 2.26

Skeletons of an antelope (A), coyote (B), horse (C) and elephant (D).

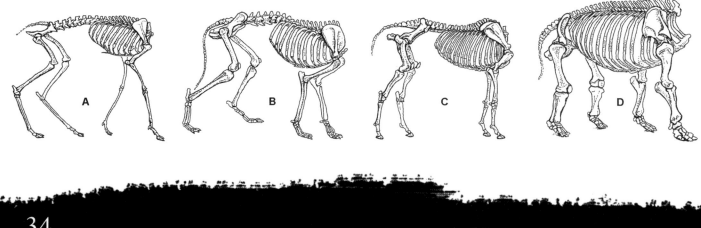

A

B

C

D

# FIGURE 2.27

A hypothetical race between some common animals.

# FIGURE 2.28

Skeletons of a *Stegosaurus* (left), *Camarasaurus* (middle), and *Struthiomimus* (right).

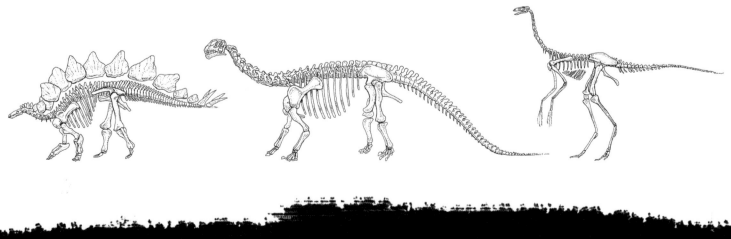

# Hatching and death on Egg Island

In our everyday life on land, we see little evidence of organisms in the act of being preserved as fossils. When living things die their bodies usually disappear in a short time. Other animals, such as bacteria and fungi, eat plants and animals. The complete decomposition of the bodies of dead organisms results in the production of gases and minerals. The "dust to dust" recycling of living things is the general rule.

Sometimes in forests under fresh and decomposing leaves, we see black carbon-rich soil. Such soils retain some of the remains of organisms, but usually there are no clues as to which decaying plants, animals, bacteria or fungi contributed to the young soil. Perhaps the fact that we normally do not see fossils form, explains why some people have trouble understanding the presence of fish, shells, and trees in rock formations around the world.

Notice whenever you go for a walk the bodies of plants and animals, the discarded parts of the organisms like leaves, shells, feces, footprints, or feathers. Perhaps you will have time to return to these sites again to observe the fate of these remnants of our time. Imagine how any one of these remains might endure for a time longer than others. Think about how fossil evidence of any one of these remains may last for a year, a century, a million years, or a thousand million years. If you ever thought about a cat waking across wet concrete, or leaf collection becoming buried in manmade airtight time capsule, think also about natural methods of preservation. The activities in this chapter are about ways fossils are preserved.

The chances of any living creature leaving its mark on Earth in the form of a fossil are remote. Despite the great odds, under certain rare circumstances, organisms—in whole, in part, or as phantom clues—may survive in fossil form. Some fossil specimens survive in such great numbers, they make up mountains of fossiliferous rock, while in other instances, only a small part of a species might be found in fossil form.

How many species (including living and extinct) have there been in the history of Earth? To estimate this number, assume there are 5,000,000 species of organisms alive today. Assume the average life span of a species is 2,000,000 years. Assume also, there is fossil evidence of life on Earth as early as 3,500,000,000 years ago, and that life originated on Earth about 3,800,000,000 year ago. It could be that as many as 2,000,000,000 species have lived on Earth.

Paleontologists have identified and named only about 150,000 fossil species, or about 0.00008% of these species calculated to have lived on Earth in all of history. Thus, if only 1 in 12,000 extinct species has been found in fossil form, it follows that few species have fossilized. Or, does it instead mean that few of the fossils have been found?

## Fossilization

Taphonomy is the science that tries to explain how living organisms, their parts, tracks, and traces become fossils in the rock of Earth. Taphonomy addresses all the biological and physical processes that transform an organism as it leaves the biosphere and becomes established in the lithosphere.

FIGURE 2.29

Dinosaur nesting site from about 75 million years ago.

The fates of organisms after death depend on many variables: where they die, how they die, the altitude of the land, the turbulence of the seawater, the fallout of a volcano, how palatable they are to other organisms, how quickly they become buried in sediments, and how mineralized is their skeletal structure. The list of conditions that favor fossilization is extensive. To get a handle on the processes by which a dying organism leaves evidence of its existence, we will illustrate the events of life and death as it occurred at the nesting sites of a species of hadrosaur during the late Cretaceous Period.

Figure 2.29 depicts the fates of dinosaur eggs in nest sites of about 75 million years ago. Similar nest sites have been found in northern China, in the basins the Rocky Mountains of Montana and Alberta, and in southern France. Included in the figure are the fates of dinosaurs whose remains were found at the nest site.

In the figure, the eggs in the nest on the hill are alive and just beginning to hatch. Notice that several babies are running around and several eggs are cracking. Bushes and boughs provide protective cover and bedding and possibly food. The nest is on high ground, possibly on an island of a continental lake or sea. Adults have been tending to the eggs. As the eggs hatch, shells are trampled, scattered and powdered by the babies. The younger members of the family then join the parents in migratory herds and return to the breeding site the following season. Predators eat some of the young; others die, rapidly decompose, and disappear. The same family will use the same nest site with a new layer of sediment again and again.

## Things to note in Figure 2.29

1. On the left slope of the egg nest hill on the shoreline surface, are the skeletal remains of a carcass of an adult dinosaur partially immersed in water. No meat remains on the scattered bones. In the coming winter storms the now disassembled bones will be separately washed down the hill into a river where several of the bones and teeth remain today in an ancient sandstone delta of an inland sea.

2. The large dead dinosaur to the right of the egg nest succumbed to old age. Her flesh was partially eaten by tyrannosaurs and other scavengers. Carrion beetles, flies, and bacteria cleaned meat from some of the bones. Small mammals are gnawing through the bones for blood-making marrow. Pterosaurs pick at the bones for meat and calcium and phosphorus salts. The exposed dinosaur was completely recycled in two days. Nothing was left to fossilize.

3. The third dinosaur had the misfortune to stumble off the shoreline into shallow water. At this spot the deep sandy sediments were fine grained, rounded, and kept in a liquid-like state by up welling spring waters. The struggling young dinosaur thus sunk into quicksand and was deeply buried before it began to decompose and disintegrate. As millions of years passed, more layers of sediment accumulated on top of the dinosaur skeleton. Bacteria and fungi cleaned out the meat. Silicon-rich volcanic ash and lava eventually covered the overlying sediments. The open spaces in the bones filled with a form of agate called red jasper. Later much of the original bone dissolved and was replaced by other forms of silicates or calcite. As time passed these petrified bones of the dinosaur were compressed, heated, and deformed by the movement of moving plates. In time the deforming bones completely lost their identity as dinosaur bones, and became an indistinguishable part of the rocks.

4. Possibly several thousand years before the events on the egg nest site that were just described, a great flood occurred in the region of the breeding grounds. The waters of the sea of the great basin rose to flood many of the nest egg sites in the breeding ground of this species of dinosaur. You can see that one site still remained under water. The eggs at this site had not yet hatched

at the time of the flood. The eggs were preserved in their original shape and appearance. A form of calcium carbonate from the water infiltrated the shell with a form of limestone. A few baby dinosaur bones have been recovered in the eggs. These dinosaur eggs were preserved by an almost instantaneous protection against destruction by predators, decomposition, and the elements of the water. Immediate burial in toxic water pickled the eggs during the first few days of their 75 million years internment as fossils in rock. Once buried sediments, and now rock, the eggs become subject to various physical and chemical changes. In this instance, the eggs became a true fossil in the original form, made of an original shell surrounding a calcium carbonate center with or without the remains of a developing dinosaur. In another instance, the shell disappeared, leaving an impression or replacement of mineral in the shape of the original specimen. The original fossil is replaced with a casting of a new chemical composition, known as pseudomorph. Whichever fate the eggs follow, the ultimate fate is deformation and the redistribution of minerals by natural geological processes.

## Questions

1. The rains that wash the land and drain the tributaries of loose bones will carry them many miles from their source in the breeding ground. Along the way they will be scattered, a tooth here and a bone there, in the sand of a river. When the river slows, a large amount of debris—including a large amount of bones—will settle into a graveyard of bones collected from a large area. Of what possible use to paleontologists would a collection of such varied bones be?

2. One dinosaur weighed about 25 tons. It accumulated this mass by eating an enormous weight of leaves of the evergreen trees. And in less than two days scavengers (dinosaurs, pterosaurs, small mammals, insects, and bacteria) returned the carcass to dust without a trace. The scavengers then die and their flesh and bones are eaten and (in rare circumstance) they are preserved as fossils. What keeps the cycle going year after year, for as long as organisms have been on Earth? (The Sun and Photosynthesis)

3. The bones of every fossil do not last forever. The bone may be replaced by agate and calcite. Pretty soon you cannot tell fossil from rock, it turns into indistinguishable rock. Is this a fact?

4. Most of the fossils of dinosaur babies come from eggs that were of the Cretaceous Period. Fossils of Jurassic babies are few, and fossils of Triassic babies are rare. Why do you think that may be so?

5. After an egg loses its shell it has no protection from soil or water. Minerals from the soil or the water replace the internal content of the egg. The internal substance may look like an egg but it really is not—it is a pseudomorph. A pseudomorph may look exactly like an egg but inside of it is nothing but mineral. How would you proceed to make a pseudomoph of an egg?

# Predation

Predation occurs when one organism feeds on another. Seashells, both fossil and recent, make excellent subjects to observe the effects of predation because many marine predators leave distinctive marks on the shells of their victims or prey. Knowledge of how to read these marks can make a trip to the beach seem like unraveling a crime story.

Moon snails are members of the family Naticidae (phylum Mollusca, class Gastropoda). They are found in marine waters all over the world, although they are more common in areas that have sandy or muddy bottoms. Moon snails have a round shell that is actually too small for them to completely withdraw their bodies (Figure 2.30).

Moon snails crawl along the surface or burrow within sand and mud in search of molluscan prey, usually clams and snails. They are very slow movers, so the prey must be equally slow in order to be run down. Once captured, the prey is enveloped in the moon snail's large foot and held while the moon snail drills a distinctive beveled hole (Figure 2.31) in the shell of the prey. It drills this hole by secreting acid onto a spot on the shell and then filing away the loosened material with its radula. Once the drill hole is complete, the moon snail inserts its

## FIGURE 2.30

Moon snail shell (left) and live moon snail (right) showing its "foot" and mantle.

## FIGURE 2.32

Shells of two species of Muricidae, which drill small, vertically sided holes in the shells of their prey.

## FIGURE 2.31

Incomplete (left) and complete (right) drill holes in shells created by moon snails.

## FIGURE 2.33

Shell clipping crab attacking a snail.

proboscis into the shell and eats the flesh of the animal.

The drilling process takes many hours during which the moon snail may be interrupted. If the prey escapes, it may have an incomplete drillhole. If the moon snail recaptures the prey, it will start drilling again, but in a new position. This may result in multiple drill holes. Therefore incomplete drill holes and multiple drill holes usually indicate that the moon snail had difficulty handling the prey.

Snails of the family Muricidae (Figure 2.32) also drill holes in shells. These snails crawl on the surface of the sediment and look for prey that also live on the surface, like oysters and mussels. The drill holes of the murex shells can be distinguished from moon snail drills because they are not beveled and have straight sides as if the hole was excavated by a power drill.

Many crabs feed on clams and snails. Some of these crabs attack the snail by carefully opening the shell along the whorl like a can opener (Figure 2.33).

Victims of these attacks have a distinctive channel cut into the shell. Survivors of such attacks can be found with healed scars in the shell (Figure 2.34).

## Activity:

Go to a beach with seashells or bring a bucket of shells into class. Look through the shells for the distinctive marks of predation. How many shells are drilled? Which of these drills are from moon snails and which, if any, are from murex shells? Calculate the percentage of drilled shells. In some places drilling can be as high as 30% of the population. Look for evidence of crab predation. How many shells have evidence of crab predation? How many survived the attack and regrew their shell? Do any of the snails show evidence of multiple attacks? Have any shells been attacked by both snails and crabs?

## FIGURE 2.34

Shell of whelk that was damaged by a crab (left) and volute snail that survived a crab attack and regrew its shell (right).

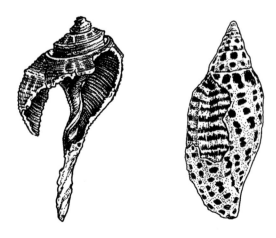

# What was the purpose of the plates on the back of *Stegosaurus*?

## FIGURE 2.35

Two living examples of animals with defensive armor; tortoise (top) and armadillo (bottom).

With its tiny head, huge plates and spiky tail, *Stegosaurus* is one of the strangest dinosaurs. The long, pointed, spear-like tail spikes were clearly for defense. But what about those plates on *Stegosaurus'* back, were they for defense too? Let's start our investigation of *Stegosaurus* by creating hypotheses about the purposes of the plates. Brainstorm some possibilities.

## FIGURE 2.37

Scared cat arching its back and extending its fur to make itself look larger to enemies.

## FIGURE 2.36

African porcupine showing its spiny defense.

## FIGURE 2.38

Puffer fish in its normal uninflated pose (bottom) and how it looks when threatened (top).

◆ Hypothesis 1: Defense/Armor. The plates serve as armor to thwart attack by predators. For example, turtles and armadillos are covered by plates (Figure 2.35).

◆ Hypothesis 2: Defense/Spikes. For example porcupines have sharp spines for protection (Figure 2.36).

◆ Hypothesis 3: Defense/Display. The plates make *Stegosaurus* look bigger to scare away predators. For example, many animals, such as cats, try to make themselves look bigger when they are scared (Figure 2.37).

Some animals may combine these traits. For example when the puffer fish is frightened, it puffs up to make itself larger and is also covered with spines (Figure 2.38).

◆ Hypothesis 4: Courtship/Display. The plates are for attracting mates. For example male peacocks have large and elaborate feathers, which seem to be solely for attracting mates (Figure 2.39).

◆ Hypothesis 5: Thermoregulation. The plates allow *Stegosaurus* to collect and radiate heat. For example elephants are large animals that live in a hot environment. They use their large ears to help radiate the heat their body produces (Figure 2.40).

Now let's make observations and predictions about these different hypotheses. Observations in this case mean looking at the characteristics of each of the traits, e.g., are porcupine quills sharp or dull? Once you have described how those traits fit a

## FIGURE 2.39

Male peacock shows off its plumage to a female

## FIGURE 2.40

Elephant and its ears, rich with blood vessels, which help radiate heat.

particular hypothesis, you test that hypothesis by making a prediction about *Stegosaurus*. For example: Porcupine spines are sharp, therefore if *Stegosaurus* plates were serving a protective function like porcupine spines do, you would expect *Stegosaurus* plates to be sharply pointed. If *Stegosaurus* plates are not sharply pointed (which they aren't) then you reject the hypothesis that the plates served as that kind of defense.

**Hypothesis 1: Defensive armor.**
Observations: Turtles and armadillos have tough platy armor that covers their entire body. The underside of turtles is covered by plates. Armadillos have a soft belly, but this vulnerable area is protected by their habit of rolling up into a ball.
Prediction: *Stegosaurus* plates will be tough and will cover the vital areas of the body.

**Hypothesis 2: Defensive spikes.**
Observations: Porcupine quills are sharp, stiff, barbed, and deter attackers by puncturing their skin.
Prediction: *Stegosaurus* plates will be strong and pointed.

**Hypothesis 3: Defensive display.**
Observations: Animals have a variety of ways to make themselves look larger. They may raise their feathers or hair or puff up their bodies. The result is a much larger looking animal. When they are not scared they usually lower their defenses and return to their normal appearance.
Prediction: *Stegosaurus* plates will make the animal look significantly larger and may be moveable.

**Hypothesis 4: Courtship display.**
Observations: In animals such as peacocks where large showy feathers attract mates, only the males have the large display feathers while the females are much drabber in appearance (this is called sexual dimorphism).
Prediction: Male *Stegosaurus* will have large plates and females will have smaller plates or no plates at all.

## FIGURE 2.41

Skeleton of *Stegosaurus.*

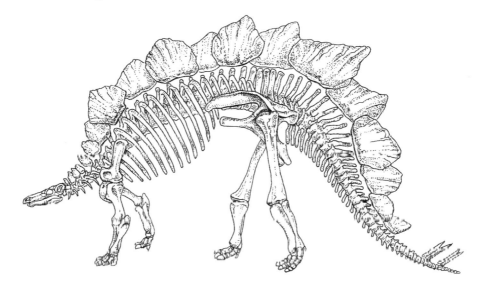

### Hypothesis 5: Thermoregulation.

Observations: Elephant ears are large and thin and full of blood vessels. Blood is then pumped into these blood vessels and heat is radiated out of the animal through the thin skin of the ear. Prediction: *Stegosaurus* plates will be large and thin and full of blood vessel holes.

Now let's make some observations on *Stegosaurus* and test these predictions (Figure 2.41):

1. *Stegosaurus* plates are not attached to the skeleton; they are embedded in the skin of the animal.
2. They occur in two rows down the back in a staggered arrangement.
3. They are largest over the hip and smallest over the neck and the middle of the tail.
4. They are thin (Figure 2.42)
5. They are more or less five-sided, and though some have "points" they are not sharp enough to puncture an attacker's skin (Figure 2.42).
6. They are full of blood vessels holes and very porous (Figure 2.42).
7. As far as we can tell (it is hard to tell the gender in dinosaurs from skeletons), *Stegosaurus* plates were not sexually dimorphic, i.e., both males and females had large plates.

## FIGURE 2.42

*Stegosaurus* plate showing its porosity and thinness.

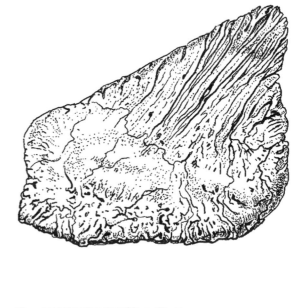

It is convenient to place these predictions and tests in a table:

| Hypothesis | Prediction | Test |
|---|---|---|
| Defensive Armor | Plates tough and cover vital areas | No: plates weak and do not cover sides |
| Defensive Spikes | Plates strong and sharp | No: plates weak and not sharp |
| Defensive Display | Plates make *Stegosaurus* look larger | Yes |
| Courtship Display | Males have plates, females don't | No: both sexes have plates |
| Thermoregulation | Plates thin and porous with many blood vessel holes | Yes |

## Conclusion:

The plates fail our tests for defensive armor, spikes, and courtship display. They meet our predictions for defensive display and thermoregulation. Can we distinguish between these two hypotheses? Let's look at the arrangement of the plates. They occur in two rows down the back in a staggered or offset pattern. If the primary purpose of the plates was to make the animal look larger, then the actual arrangement would not be important, i.e., they could occur in a single row or in two rows without overlap. However the arrangement may be important if the plates serve as heat collectors or radiators. Some scientists did an experiment in which they made metal models to simulate three different plate arrangements. One model had a single long fin running down the back, the second model had two rows of plates arranged directly opposite each other, and the third model had two rows of plates arranged in a staggered or offset pattern as in *Stegosaurus*. The surface areas of the plates were the same for all three models. They heated the models to the same temperature, put them in a wind tunnel and then measured how fast each of them radiated heat. The third model, with the plates in two staggered rows, radiated heat the fastest. This further supports the hypothesis that the plates were used for thermoregulation. But we still can't definitively state the purpose of the *Stegosaurus* plates. While *Stegosaurus* is the only member of an entire group of armored dinosaurs with flat plates in two rows, it is difficult to imagine it had a unique metabolism from all its relatives. The exact purpose of the plates remains an unanswered mystery.

## Final Note:

All scientific hypotheses are tentative. A new analysis with more information may yield a different result. Also, many body parts may serve multiple functions. The claws of a bear can be used for digging but they also make formidable weapons. Likewise, the plates on *Stegosaurus* may have served several purposes, e.g., heat regulation *and* defensive display.

# Mass Extinction and Meteor Collisions With Earth

## Introduction

Earth is constantly bombarded by rocks from space. Rock sizes range from specks of dust, to pea-size pebbles, to boulders of many tons, to asteroids up to several kilometers in diameter and millions of tons in mass (Figure 3.1). Dust produces the often seen meteors or shooting stars, and boulders produce fireballs. The rare asteroids and comets cause catastrophic damage to Earth.

Most large meteors originate in the asteroid belt in orbit between Jupiter and Mars. They escape this orbit when asteroid collisions occur, or when strong gravitational forces from Jupiter perturb them into new Earth-crossing orbits. Space rocks may also come from the Moon or inner planets after major collisions with bolides (large meteors) on these nearby celestial bodies. For example 34 meteorites on Earth have been identified as having a Martian origin. Some space rocks are parts of comets that originate in outer regions of the solar system and move in elliptical orbits around the Sun.

Like the rocks of Earth, meteorites resemble in composition the core, mantle, and crust of Earth. In general, meteorites are either composed of iron-nickel or of stone... but there are stony irons. Even among the irons and the stones there are classes and subclasses. Stones are more abundant than irons. However, large iron meteors resist burning and breaking up as they enter the atmosphere better than do stones. The history of life on Earth is characterized by long periods of slow change punctuated by moments of rapid geological change. These rapid changes in Earth's environments are attributed by some scientists to the effects of asteroid collisions. In such extreme geological moments mass extinctions occur, followed by adaptive radiations of survivors.

## Causes of extinctions

Over 99% of all the species that have ever lived are now extinct. This statement seems outrageous on the face of it, but let's work it out. The average geological life span of a species is about 5 million years. Complex organisms large enough to be seen with the naked eye have been around for over 500 million years. Thus, there have been over a hundred "generations" of species on the planet, Earth on average replacing its organisms with new species every 5 million years. Therefore over 99% of all species that have lived are now extinct. Put in this simplistic way, extinction is a natural process that occurs all the time, right along with speciation or the evolution of new species.

Topic: Dinosaur Extinction
Go to: www.scilinks.org
Code: AP007

## FIGURE 3.1

Meteor entering Earth's atmosphere.

# FIGURE 3.2

Geological time scale

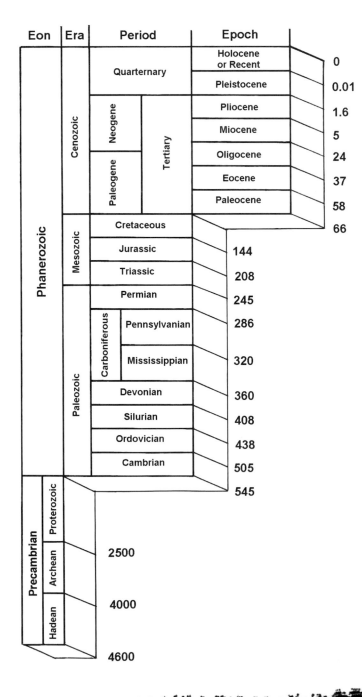

| Eon | Era | Period | Epoch | |
|-----|-----|--------|-------|---|
| Phanerozoic | Cenozoic | Quarternary | Holocene or Recent | 0 |
| | | | Pleistocene | 0.01 |
| | | Neogene / Tertiary | Pliocene | 1.6 |
| | | | Miocene | 5 |
| | | | Oligocene | 24 |
| | | Paleogene / Tertiary | Eocene | 37 |
| | | | Paleocene | 58 |
| | Mesozoic | Cretaceous | | 66 |
| | | Jurassic | | 144 |
| | | Triassic | | 208 |
| | Paleozoic | Permian | | 245 |
| | | Carboniferous / Pennsylvanian | | 286 |
| | | Carboniferous / Mississippian | | 320 |
| | | Devonian | | 360 |
| | | Silurian | | 408 |
| | | Ordovician | | 438 |
| | | Cambrian | | 505 |
| | | | | 545 |
| Precambrian | Proterozoic | | | 2500 |
| | Archean | | | 4000 |
| | Hadean | | | 4600 |

But let's look at extinction in more detail.

Paleontologists divide extinctions into two broad categories: background extinctions and mass extinctions. Background extinctions occur continuously as a result of environmental changes, predation, competition, etc. They probably occur at a rate of 10's to 100's of species per year. Generally species that go extinct in this fashion have been replaced by the evolution of new species so that overall diversity, or the total number of species, has remained stable or increased. Mass extinctions are unusual in that they involve very large numbers (millions) of species, of very different kinds (e.g., clams, dinosaurs, plants) dying within a relatively short time. What is a short time? To a geologist, a short time means around 1–2 million years. Although some extinctions probably occurred over much shorter intervals, say hundreds to thousands of years, it is difficult to tell time with this much precision in the rock record. Often all we know is that the extinction took less than a million years.

Mass extinctions mark turning points in evolution. The biggest extinctions not only killed a lot of species, they also altered the biological landscape so that the organisms and communities that took the place of the extinct ones were radically different. Geologists divide Earth's history into intervals called eons, eras, and periods (Figure 3.2). The Phanerozoic Eon, which stared about 545 million years ago, is divided into 3 eras and 12 periods. During the Phanerozoic Eon there were five major mass extinctions and many smaller ones. The two biggest extinctions occurred at the Paleozoic-Mesozoic and Mesozoic-Cenozoic boundaries, and most other major extinctions occured at or near period boundaries. This is no coincidence. The geologic time scale was divided and named based on the great changes in life brought about by the extinctions.

The extinction at the Mesozoic-Cenozoic boundary occurred about 65 million years ago. Its most famous victims were the dinosaurs, but many other groups went extinct including swimming and flying reptiles, many groups of mollusks, and many species of marine microplankton. Over half of all species went extinct at this time. What caused this extinction? There is a great deal of evidence that suggests it was caused by an asteroid impact. This evidence includes a giant impact crater buried beneath the surface of the Yucatán Peninsula in Central America. In addition, a variety of particles and elements that are indicative of an impact were deposited in rocks in the same sedimentary layer as the extinctions.

What were the effects of the impact of this asteroid? Given an estimate of the mass and speed of the asteroid, the effects can be modeled (see Activities 2–4 in this chapter). For instance, if we assume the asteroid was 10 km in diameter (based on the size of the crater beneath the Yucatán Peninsula), and was traveling about 30 km per second (about the average speed of meteorites), and had the density of an average asteroid, then the energy released by its impact would be equal to about 10 billion 15-kiloton (about the size of the atomic bomb dropped on Hiroshima) atomic bombs. Or put another way, an energy release equivalent to covering every square meter of land on Earth with two tons of TNT. The effect of this much energy released in one place is fantastic. There is evidence of huge tsunamis emanating from the impact site and striking all around the Gulf of Mexico. There is evidence that the heat of the explosion ignited forest fires around the world. The smoke from these fires and the dust thrown into the atmosphere from the impact probably shut out sunlight and darkened the surface for months. The lack of light had disastrous effects on plant life, which in turn affected the herbivorous animals that ate the plants and then the carnivores that ate the herbivores. By destroying the plants at the base of the food chain, a vast chain reaction was set in motion that resulted in many of the world's species dying out.

Though the evidence is strong for an impact at the Mesozoic-Cenozoic extinction, evidence for impact as a cause is weak or lacking for most of the other extinctions. There have been many other causes proposed for these extinctions including massive volcanic eruptions, changes in sea level, and climatic cooling. Periods of widespread volcanism put huge amounts of carbon dioxide into the atmosphere. Carbon dioxide is a greenhouse gas, meaning it helps trap heat from the sun in our atmosphere, and sudden large inputs of this gas could quickly raise global temperatures. Overheating of Earth can cause extinctions by melting the polar ice caps and raising the sea level, slowing ocean circulation and upwelling, and by simply making it too warm for many species to survive. New species would evolve to live in these new oceans and in the warmer temperatures, but not before extinctions had occurred. There is some evidence that the Permian-Triassic extinction was the result of global warming and large expanses of volcanic lava erupted at about this time. Sudden cooling can also cause extinctions. It is well known that fewer species of plants and animals live in polar and temperate regions than in the tropics. So a climatic event that turns a largely tropical world into a temperate or polar one will cause many extinctions. There is a great deal of evidence that suggests that extinctions at the end of the Ordovician Period and in the Mid-Cenozoic were caused by global cooling. Sea

Topic: Asteroids
Go to: www.scilinks.org
Code: AP008

level changes can cause extinction by drowning a previously dry continent, and thus killing the animals that lived on the continent, or by exposing an area that was previously underwater and thereby killing the marine life that inhabited the former ocean. At several times in Earth's past, vast areas of the continents have been flooded or exposed. Half of North America was underwater at some time during the age of the dinosaurs. To make matters more complicated, both global warming and cooling will affect sea level by melting or growing the polar ice caps, so several different causes may act in concert to cause an extinction.

## TEACHER'S NOTES:

### Answers to questions in Activity 2:

QUESTION 1:

Answer: The mass of the meteor can be calculated by multiplying its volume by its density. Let's assume the meteor is a sphere. The volume of a sphere is $4/3\pi r^3$. Iron/nickel has a density of about 8 grams per cubic centimeter. Therefore the mass of the meteor = $(4/3)(3.1416)(0.05cm)^3$ $(8g/cm^3)$=0.0042g or 0.0000042kg. The kinetic energy can be calculated with the equation KE = $\frac{1}{2} mv^2$ = $(0.05)(0.0000042kg)(32000m/sec)^2$ = 2150 Joules. Energy released is the equivalent of 0.51 calories, about the energy you get from four ounces of diet soda.

QUESTION 2:

Answer: Convert tons to kilograms: 1 kilogram = 2.2 pounds, therefore 50 tons = (50 tons)(2000lbs/ton)/2.2kgs/lb = 45454.5 kg

KE = $(0.5)(45454.5kg)(32000 m/sec)^2$ = $2.33 \times 10^{13}$ joules. To help put this in perspective, a thousand tons of TNT (1 kiloton) has an energy yield $4.2 \times 10^{12}$ Joules. Therefore $2.33 \times 10^{13}$ joules is about the yield of 5,000 tons of TNT.

QUESTION 3:

Answer: Convert miles to centimeters and find the volume of the asteroid: 6 miles = (6mi)(5280ft/mi)(30.5cm/ft)

= 966240cm.

Volume = $4/3\pi r^3$

 = $(4/3)(3.1416)(483120cm)^3$

= $4.72 \times 1017$ cubic cm.

(Volume)(density) = mass

Mass = $(4.72 \times 10^{17}cc)(8g/cc)$

 = $3.8 \times 10^{18}g$ or $3.8 \times 10^{15}kg$.

KE = $(0.5)(3.8 \times 10^{15}kg)(32000m/sec)^2$

= $1.95 \times 10^{24}$ joules. (Additional energy released after impact originates from such exothermic reactions as the burning of trees and sulfur.)

Let's put $1.95 \times 10^{24}$ joules in perspective: The atomic bomb dropped on Hiroshima has a yield of 20 kilotons of TNT. Therefore, the Hiroshima A-bomb had an energy yield of $(20)(4.2 \times 10^{12}$ joules) = $8.4 \times 10^{13}$ joules. If we divide this figure into the kinetic energy of our six-mile asteroid, we find that its impact would release the energy equivalent of 23 *billion* A-bombs. That is enough to strap four A-bombs onto every man, woman and child on the planet.

QUESTION4:

Answer: KE = (0.5)(63000tons)(2000lbs/ton)/2.2lbs/kg)

$(10mi/sec)(5280ft/mi)(0.305m/ft)^2$ = $7.4 \times 10^{15}$ joules

This is the energy equivalent of 90 Hiroshima atomic bombs.

# Searching for micrometeorites

Researchers estimate between 100 million and 8 billion tons of micrometeorites fall on Earth annually (Figure 3.3). Much of this dust is magnetic iron-nickel that can be collected and examined.

## Procedures:

1. Collect several spoons full of dirt from the base of a drain spout or a rain gutter of a house or other building. Tile roofs are best since they do not produce other particles, and they drain well. Pour the dirt into a cup. Dry the dirt. Place a strong magnet in a plastic bag. Run the bagged magnet through the collected dirt allowing magnetic dirt to cling to the plastic bag. Release the magnetic dirt into a white dish. Use a microscope to search for spherical or smooth objects that may have flamed and melted when they entered the atmosphere, forming droplets as they cooled. An alternative technique is to use a piece of transparent tape to pick up the magnetic particles from the white dish, and view the strip with a microscope.

2. Catch micrometeorites on a greased slide. Thinly coat a microscope slide with petroleum jelly. Heat the slide to obtain a thin uniform film. Expose the slide to the sky where it will be undisturbed for 24 hours. Examine the slide under high magnification. Look for spherical shiny bodies. Estimate the number of similar particles falling on the entire Earth in one day, noting that the total surface area of Earth is $5.10 \times 10^{18} \text{cm}^2$. Collect a sample of particles settling from the air onto a tray for a day or more. Weigh a small magnet to 0.1 mg. Sweep the tray with the magnet to pick up all magnetic particles. Weigh the magnet with iron particles. The difference is the weight of presumed micrometeorites. Remove magnetic particles from magnet with transparent tape. Using the values of weight or particles, area of the tray, and the area of Earth's surface, calculate the mass of magnetic micrometeorites falling to Earth each year.

3. Test your micrometeorites for nickel metal. Since elemental nickel hardly ever occurs in terrestrial rock, the detection of nickel in a rock is a good test for a meteorite. Wearing goggles, rubber gloves, and working in a hood, dissolve, in separate test tubes, less than a gram of meteoritic rock, some iron, some nickel, and suspected micrometeorites in heated concentrated HCl. When dissolved, add a few drops of concentrated nitric acid. Immediately add several drops of citric acid to prevent the iron from precipitating. Neutralize with $NH_4OH$. Filter the solution if it is not clear. Test for nickel by adding a few drops of a 1% alcohol solution of dimethylglyoxime. When nickel is present the solution turns a bright cherry red.

## MATERIALS:

- spoon
- cup
- zip-lock bag
- magnet
- magnifying lens
- microscope and slides
- petroleum jelly
- HCl
- nitric acid
- $NH_4OH$
- citric acid
- dimethylglyoxime
- heater
- test tubes
- medicine droppers
- beakers
- funnels
- filter paper

## FIGURE 3.3

Micrometeorites; scale bar on left is 200 microns, scale bar on right is 100 microns.

# Calculating the energy of incoming rocks from space

## MATERIALS:

- calculator
- balance and weights
- real or substitute meteorite

Topic: Meteors
Go to: www.scilinks.org
Code: AP009

## Procedure:

You can calculate the energy of a moving object when you know the mass and velocity of the object. Use the equation: Kinetic Energy (in joules) = (0.50)(mass in kilograms)(velocity in meters/second squared), or K.E. = $\frac{1}{2} mv^2$.

For example, suppose a 60-gram ball falling at a velocity of 2 meters per second splashes into a pond. How much energy was transferred from the ball to the pond at impact?

Answer: K.E. = (0.50)(.06kg)(2meters/second)$^2$ = 0.12 joules.

Since there are 4180 joules in a (food) calorie, the energy released by this collision is equivalent to 0.0000029 calories

Let us now calculate the energies of three sizes of rocks from space as they collide with Earth.

1. Most meteors (shooting stars) are mere specks, the size of grains of sand, when they crash into Earth's atmosphere. But their energy is great enough to produce bright lights that streak across the sky. Suppose a particular micrometeorite entered the atmosphere as an iron/nickel sphere with a diameter of 1.0mm at a velocity of 32,000 meters/second. How much energy is released?

2. Suppose a fireball-producing meteor with a mass of 50 tons enters the atmosphere at 32,000 meters/second. How much energy will it release?

3. Suppose an iron/nickel asteroid six miles in diameter crashes into Earth at a velocity of 32,000 meters/second. How much energy of motion does it release to Earth?

4. The Arizona meteor crater formed in an instant about 50,000 years ago (Figure 3.4). Although the meteorite was vaporized on impact, scientists estimate that the meteorite had a mass of 63,000 tons, a diameter of about 80 feet and a velocity of 10 miles per second. About how much energy was transferred from meteorite to Earth during this collision?

## FIGURE 3.4

Meteor Crater in Arizona.

# Modeling impact craters

## Introduction

A look at the surfaces of inner planets, moons, and asteroids in our solar system reveals numerous scars of meteor impacts. Even Earth shows evidence of extensive cratering during the past 600 million years. Since Earth is subject to continuous weathering, craters tend to fill up and erode into obscurity faster than those on our airless moon or the planet Mercury. Scientists have a lot of questions about how impact craters form. True impacts are rarely seen. Most studies of cratering are limited to simulations of impacts in laboratories using "meteorites" of small mass and low velocity. In this activity you will be working in such a laboratory.

## MATERIALS:

- ◆ sandbox
- ◆ sand
- ◆ crushed limestone
- ◆ assorted steel spheres
- ◆ electromagnet
- ◆ switch
- ◆ ruler
- ◆ video camera

## Procedures:

1. Fill a sandbox (about 50cm by 100cm square), or a tiny tot's wading pool, with fine grain sand to a depth of about 30cm. Support a rod about 2 meters above the sand. Fix an electromagnet above the sand with an off/on switch on the line (Figure 3.5). The magnet should be strong enough to support steel spheres of the various masses available.

2. Release a steel ball (by turning off the electromagnet) so it falls freely into the sand. Record the mass of the ball, the diameter of the ball, the height the ball falls, the diameter of the crater made, the depth of the crater, and the depth of the penetration of the ball into the sand.

3. Repeat the collisions using steel spheres of different sizes. Record all data. Search for relationships between masses and the results of the impacts.

4. Now repeat the tests changing the height the sphere falls. Calculate the energy of impact by measuring the mass of the sphere and its velocity at impact using K.E. (in Joules) = $1/2mv^2$. Terminal velocity of a free falling mass = 2gh. The kinetic energy of a 50g sphere falling from a height of 2.5m is $(0.5)(0.05kg)(7m/sec) = 0.175$ Joules. What relationship can you see between energy and crater diameter?

## FIGURE 3.5

Apparatus for simulating impacts.

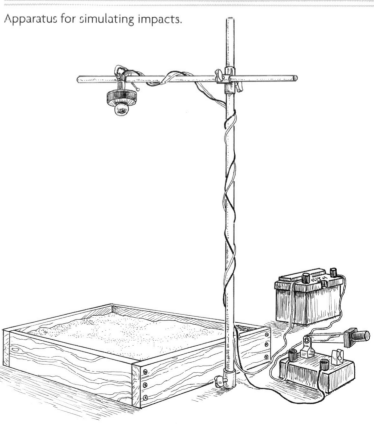

ANALYSIS:

| Attributes | | |
|---|---|---|
| Mass of sphere | Trial 1: | |
| | Trial 2: | |
| | Trial 3: | |
| | Trial 4: | |
| | Trial 5: | |
| Height above sand | Trial 1: | |
| | Trial 2: | |
| | Trial 3: | |
| | Trial 4: | |
| | Trial 5: | |
| Crater diameter | Trial 1: | |
| | Trial 2: | |
| | Trial 3: | |
| | Trial 4: | |
| | Trial 5: | |
| Crater depth | Trial 1: | |
| | Trial 2: | |
| | Trial 3: | |
| | Trial 4: | |
| | Trial 5: | |
| Depth of penetration | Trial 1: | |
| | Trial 2: | |
| | Trial 3: | |
| | Trial 4: | |
| | Trial 5: | |
| Sand/ limestone | Trial 1: | |
| | Trial 2: | |
| | Trial 3: | |
| | Trial 4: | |
| | Trial 5: | |
| Eject patterns | Trial 1: | |
| | Trial 2: | |
| | Trial 3: | |
| | Trial 4: | |
| | Trial 5: | |

5. If you become interested in studying ejecta patterns, you may want to substitute pulverized limestone for sand. The limestone holds together better than sand, and thus shows rays, secondary craters, and blankets or ejecta. The patterns of rays formed around craters can be more easily studied by sprinkling iron filings over the surface of the sand or limestone before impact.

Preparing sand with alternating layers of colored sand enables the researcher to trace the ejection of sand at various depths from the impact site. Unfortunately the test mixes the sand, preventing one from reusing the sand in layers experiments. You should videotape these one-time events. Videotaping impacts is useful in observing the details of crater formation. Videotaping has the additional advantage of enabling the viewer to see events in slow motion.

Crater specialists have a lot of questions to answer. One of their biggest problems is figuring out the size of a space rock from the diameter of the crater it left behind. From your laboratory experiment, what would you guess was the size of a meteorite that made the 1.2 kilometer in diameter crater in Arizona 50,000 years ago?

# What happens when the energy of an asteroid or comet is released in the rock and atmosphere of Earth?

## Procedure:

Table 3.1 records the diameters, locations, and ages of selected craters.

1. Search for a relationship between these impact craters and events in the history of life on Earth comparing them to the Geological Time Scale in Figure 3.2.

2. What events occurred around the times these large craters known as astroblemes or "star wounds" formed on Earth's surface.

3. Close your eyes and imagine the crash of the asteroid or comet on South Africa about 250 million years ago. Where did all the energy of the giant meteorite go? How did the solid Earth respond physically? How did the atmosphere respond? What happened to the ice caps? The plants, animals, and other organisms? What percentage of living species do you think became extinct? Why do you think that many of the species which evolved after the cataclysm were different from those that lived before?

4. Create a piece of art that communicates the role of asteroid collisions in the evolution of Earth and life.

## TABLE 3.1

Selected List of Authenticated Impact Craters Worldwide.

More than 150 impact craters have been identified worldwide and newly identified craters continue to be added to the list each year. Almost all the structures exhibit a variety of evidence pointing to impact origin. Most are visible on the surface. The ten listed here are among the largest or the best known on the planet. The type of evidence is tabulated as follows: (1) shock metamorphism, (2) coesite or stishovite (rocks that formed by impact); (3) shatter cones; (4) raised rim or a central uplift; (5) ring structure; (6) shattered rock breccia or a breccia lens; (7) impact melt or impactite glass; (8) meteorites or meteoritic oxide.

| Name & Location | Diameter (miles) | Evidence (type) | Age (MYA) | Visible on Surface? |
|---|---|---|---|---|
| Acraman (Australia) | 55.9 | 6 | <450 | Yes |
| Chesapeake Bay (Virginia, USA) | 52.8 | 1 | 35.5 + 0.6 | No |
| Chicxulub (Yucatan, Mexico) | 112 | 1, 6 | 64.98 + 0.05 | No |
| Kara-Kul (Tajikistan) | 40.4 | 2, 4, 6, 7 | <5 | No |
| Manicouagan Lake (Quebec, Ontario) | 62.1 | 3, 5 | 214 + 1 | Yes |
| Meteor Crater (Arizona, USA) | 0.74 | 1, 2, 3, 6 | 0.049 + .003 | Yes |
| Poigai Basin (Siberia, Russia) | 62.1 | 2, 6, 7 | 35 + 5 | Yes |
| Ries Basin (Bayern, Germany) | 14.8 | 1, 2, 3, 4, 6, 7 | 15 + 1 | Yes |
| Sudbury Structure (Ontario, Canada) | 155 | 1, 3 | 1850 + 3 | Yes |
| Vredefort Ring (South Africa) | 186 | 2, 3, 6 | 2023 + 4 | Yes |

# How Are Fossils Collected and Prepared?

Sometimes fossils occur in beds that are rich enough and are preserved well enough that little needs to be done except pick them up. Other times more work is involved with both collection and preparation. In this chapter we present three activities that focus on specific fossil collection and preparation techniques. Activity 1 (Preparing a fossil fish) guides students through the process of cleaning a fossil fish and preparing it for display. Spectacularly well-preserved fossil fish from the Eocene Epoch (about 50 million years ago) of Wyoming are on display in museums around the world. Slabs containing these fish are available from several sources listed in this book at very reasonable prices and by following the procedures outlined in Activity 1, students can have their own specimen for display.

Frequently, museums make reproductions of fossils for display or for sale. Sometimes fossils such as footprints cannot actually be removed from their site and a reproduction must be made in the field. Activity 2 (Making fossil replicas) describes the processes for making molds and casts of body fossils and footprints. Using these techniques students can make their own replicas of fossils and also make casts of modern animal tracks on mud flats or riverbanks.

Everybody has seen macrofossils such as dinosaur bones or petrified wood, but few have seen microfossils that are visible only under a microscope. Yet microfossils are extremely important for helping to correlate sedimentary layers in the search for oil or for decoding Earth's ancient climates from deep sea cores. Microfossils are both beautiful and abundant, and are a fascinating aspect of a normally unseen world. Activity 3 (Microfossils) explains how to find, collect, and display microfossils.

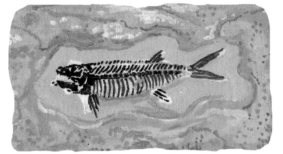

# Preparing a fossil fish

## MATERIALS:

- ◆ slab containing fish fossil
- ◆ dissecting needle
- ◆ lamp
- ◆ gum eraser
- ◆ brush
- ◆ magnifying glass

In Western Wyoming, at the site of an ancient freshwater lake (called Fossil Lake, it dates from the Eocene Epoch, about 50 million years ago), there is a rich deposit of fish fossils. They occur in limestone 18 inches thick and just below the surface, in slabs that are easily cut and removed from the rock. Oftentimes the rock surface will show signs of the fossil fish. Other times the rock may not reveal a fossil underneath, but the fish is still there. The site is located in the national park called Fossil Butte National Monument in Kemmerer, Wyoming.

Figure 4.1 shows a group of quarry men working at the site of the "18 inch" rock. They are cutting and removing the thin slabs of fossil fish at a quarry near Kemmerer, Wyoming. You can obtain a slab of a fish by writing to one of the sellers whose name and address appears at the end of this activity.

## FIGURE 4.1

Workers removing slabs of limestone bearing fossil fish at a quarry near Kemmerer, Wyoming

## FIGURE 4.2

Materials needed for excavating fossil fish.

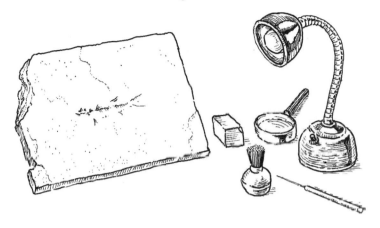

## FIGURE 4.3

Two techniques NOT to use with the dissecting needle.

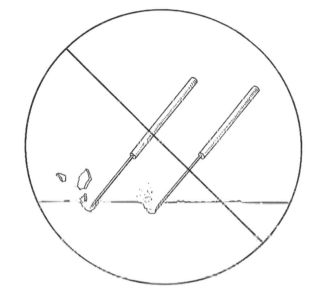

You can find fish of various ages and lengths, from fish still in eggs to some in excess of one meter in length. There are 14 different genera and 20 different species found in Fossil Lake, from small fossil herring to the large gar (1.65 meters). In addition to the fish in the freshwater lake, there are snakes, turtles, alligators, birds, bats, and palm leaves, but they are quite rare compared to the fish. At other depths in the Fossil Lake limestone, fish are not nearly as abundant as in the "18 inch" layer but they still show the diversity. It is thought that at the time the "18 inch" layer was being deposited there were many mass fish deaths. To learn more about the fish and other organisms found in Fossil Lake, you might refer to the well-illustrated references of the fish of Fossil Lake in the list of readings.

Your first time, uncovering your fish will take up to 30 hours of work, so work in short increments and enjoy your effort. If you are patient, your fossil fish may come out in excellent condition. You can exhibit your fish in a variety of ways: Frame it: hang it on a loop; or just lay it out. Professional preparers become so adept at it they can do a fish in less than an hour.

## FIGURE 4.4

Uncovering the fossil in the slab.

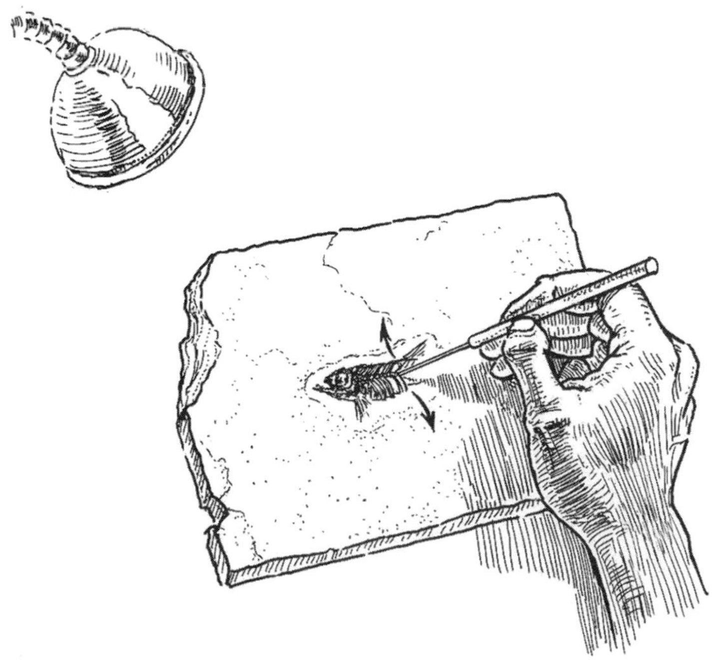

## FIGURE 4.5

The finished product; a completely cleaned fossil fish.

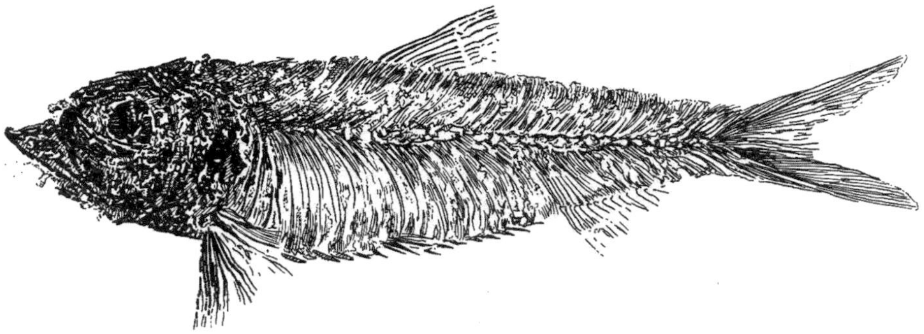

## Suggested reading:

Grande, L. 1984. Paleontology of the Green River formation, with a review of the fish fauna. *Geological Survey of Wyoming Bulletin* 63: 1–333.

Jackson, R. W. 1988. *The Fish of Fossil Lake: The Story of Fossil Butte National Monument.* Dinosaur Nature Association and Natural Park Service.

Piccini, S. 1997. *Fossils of the Green River Formation.* Italy: Geofin, s.r.l. Publishing House.

## FIGURE 4.6

Two ways to mount your fossil fish.

## Supplies:

Slabs may be purchased from the following companies:

Creative Dimensions
P.O. 1393
Bellingham, WA 98225

James and Carolyn Tinsky
Green River Geological Laboratories
Warfield, Wyoming

Carl and Shirley Ulrich
Fossil Station #308
Kemmerer, Wyoming 83101
*www.ulrichsfossilgallery.com*

# Making fossil replicas

Making replicas of fossils is simple and can be done with easily obtained materials. The simplest replica is to make a cast of a fossil from a natural mold. When a fossil is buried and the surrounding sediment turns to rock, sometimes the fossil is dissolved by groundwater seeping through the rock leaving a mold (see figure 4.7. A mold is the external impression or cavity left by the fossil, while a cast is the filling of the mold). A temporary cast of this fossil can be made by squeezing modeling clay or Play-Doh into the cavity.

A more permanent cast can be made by filling the cavity with liquid latex, which can be purchased from a latex supply company. First moisten the cavity by squirting water into the hole and then fill with latex. Let it dry overnight and then pull the cast out of the cavity. The flexibility of the latex allows it to stretch and permits casting of fairly complicated shapes.

You can also reproduce three-dimensional fossils. First use the liquid latex mentioned above to make a mold of the fossil. Do this by taking a cheap paintbrush and coating the surface of the fossil with a thin layer of latex (Figure 4.7). Spread the latex out beyond the base to make a flange, which will be useful later. One side of the

## FIGURE 4.7

Steps in making a mold and cast of a fossil.

## FIGURE 4.8

Making a mold of a footprint.

fossil must be left uncoated so that the mold can be filled with plaster later. Allow to dry overnight, then brush on another coat. Be sure to thoroughly wash out the brush with soap and water after each coat. Repeat this process until you create a latex mold about 2–3 mm thick, which you peel off the original. Moisten the mold with water and then place mold in a can or other kind of stand. Fill with wet plaster of paris (Figure 4.7). Tap the filled mold sharply with a pencil or ruler to shake loose any bubbles that may have formed along the sides of the mold. Allow the plaster to set and harden (at least 30 minutes) and then peel off the mold from the cast.

Once the cast has dried completely (usually several days) you can paint it to look like a natural fossil and then coat it with a very dilute mixture of water and white glue (such as Elmer's Glue). The diluted glue should be thin enough that it soaks into the plaster easily. This coat will strengthen the cast and keep it from staining.

To make a mold of a track, first make a dam about 1/2 to 1 inch high all around the track with clay (Figure 4.8). Brush oil or rub a thin layer of Vaseline over the track and then fill with wet plaster of paris. After the plaster has set, pry the mold off of the track. You can follow the same procedure to make a mold of a recent track in sand or mud. In this case however you do not need to coat the track with oil or grease but simply pour it onto the sediment.

# Microfossils

The term microfossil means "small fossil" which is usually defined as smaller than 1 millimeter in diameter. Some can be seen with a magnifying glass; others require microscopes to view them. Microfossils are very important in paleontology because they can be abundantly preserved in small samples such as ocean cores where larger fossils may be rare. Microfossils are often very widespread because ocean currents can carry them around the world. This wide distribution makes them excellent for correlating rocks on different continents. The organisms that comprise microfossils can be very simple or complex. Some are simple single-celled organisms such as diatoms, radiolaria, and foraminifera. Others, such as ostracods, are complex multicelled animals. And still others, such as mollusks, are the larval or juvenile stages of organisms that are much larger as adults. In this section we will review some of the common organisms that make up the microfossils and how you can collect them.

There are a huge number of species of microorganisms. Phytoplankton, the photosynthesizing single-celled organisms that float in the seas, are the basis for the oceanic food chain and are very numerous and diverse. Zooplankton, the tiny animals that float in the ocean, often eat phytoplankton and are themselves food for many larger animals. In this activity, we will focus only on small organisms that have shells and are commonly preserved as fossils and that can be seen with a magnifying glass or a low power microscope.

Diatoms are single-celled photosynthetic organisms that live in both fresh and salt water. They may make up the bulk of the phytoplankton in some parts of the ocean and the concentrated deposits of their shells form diatomaceous earth. Their shell is made of silica (glass) and is structured like a pillbox, with two halves, one of which fits inside the other. They are very intricate and beautiful (Figure 4.9). You can observe living diatoms as well as nonmineralized phytoplankton and zooplankton by making your own plankton net (see instructions for making inexpensive plankton net below).

## FIGURE 4.9

Some representative examples of diatoms.

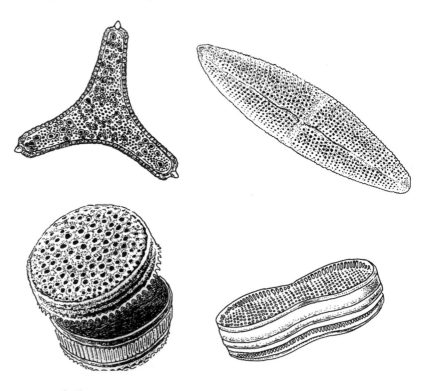

### FIGURE 4.10

Some representative examples of foraminifera.

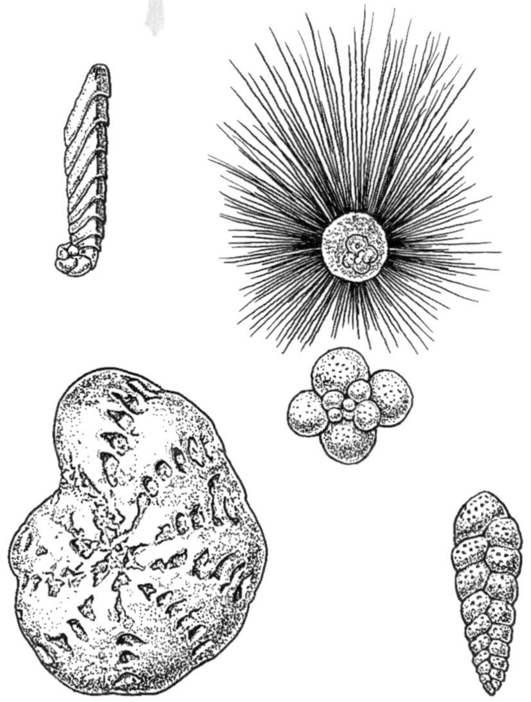

Foraminifera, or "forams," are single-celled organisms that are much like amoebas with shells. The shells are usually made of calcium carbonate, but may also be constructed of sand grains or other particles that have been glued together. The shells consist of one or more chambers and comprise a wide variety of shapes (Figure 4.10). Forams live inside their shell and capture food by means of fine hair-like extensions of their protoplasm that extend through small holes in the shell. Some forams look much like small snails, but forams are smaller than most juvenile snails and snail shells do not have chambers.

Ostracods are very small crustaceans (related to shrimp and crabs) that live inside a bivalved shell that looks like a small peanut shell or kidney bean (Figure 4.11). They are multicelled and much more complex than diatoms and forams in that they have internal organs, legs, antennae, etc. The shells separate after death. The shells are composed of calcium carbonate and may be smooth or ornamented.

Mollusks are also complex multicelled animals that comprise the Gastropoda (snails), Bivalvia (clams), Cephalopoda (squids and octopus), as well as some other groups. Most mollusks are larger than 1.00 mm, but their juvenile and larval shells are often found in

### FIGURE 4.11

Internal and external views of a living ostracod (left) and two examples of ostracod shells (right).

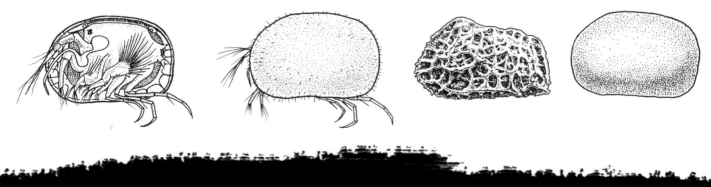

sediment along with other microfossils. Forams sometimes bear a superficial resemblance to gastropods, but gastropods do not have chambers like forams (Figure 4.12).

## Preparation of microfossil samples:

Microfossils are usually present in fine-grained sedimentary rocks, such as shales, siltstones, and clays that also contain macrofossils. They may also be present in sands, but since they are the same size as sand granules, they are usually outnumbered by the much more numerous mineral grains and difficult to find. If you are lucky enough to have unconsolidated (not yet turned to rock) fossil-bearing sediments nearby, you can easily look for microfossils yourself. Excavate a small piece of the sediment and let it dry completely. Then put it in a jar with hot water and a tablespoon of baking soda. If the sediment has clay in it, the baking soda and hot water will help separate the clay grains. Let the mixture sit for about 30 minutes. When the sample is completely liquefied, wash it through two sieves, one made out of window screen (which has openings of about 1 mm) on top and one make out of cheesecloth or panty hose underneath. The top screen will remove the coarser particles, making it easier to see the microfossils, and the bottom screen will let the clay and finer material pass through. Your microfossils will be concentrated on the cheesecloth or pantyhose. Let the material dry and then examine it under a 10–30 power binocular microscope.

## Collecting microfossils:

Because they are so small, microfossils are difficult to handle. One good way to pick them up is to use a fine tip camel hair paintbrush (a 00000 or "5 zero" size works well). Moisten the tip with water and touch it to the fossil. The water in the brush will pick up the fossil by surface tension and you can then transfer it to a small petri dish. You can also make a permanent mounting on cardboard or paper. Take an index card or piece of stiff paper (black or another dark color is best for highlighting the fossils) and rub it with a water-soluble glue stick (e.g. Pritt or UHU brands). After the glue has dried, pick up the microfossil with a moistened brush as described above. Gently place the fossil onto the glued surface while at the same time working the wet brush tip into the glue to soften it and hold the fossil. Arrange the fossils according to species and group them in lines across the card.

## FIGURE 4.12

Relative sizes of typical forams and ostracods in relation to larval and juvenile mollusks in a microfossil sample.

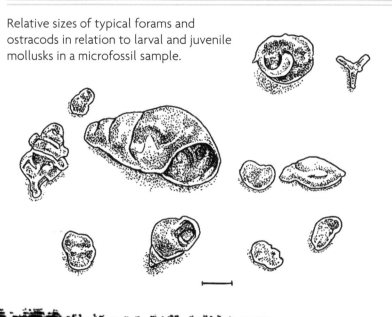

# How Can You Tell the Age of Earth?

One of the greatest discoveries of the science of geology was that Earth is very old, about 4.6 billion years old. This number is astonishingly big. So big that it is a little difficult to convey its magnitude to students. In the activity in this chapter we present a table of measurements that can be used to construct a model of the age of Earth and some of the most important events in its history, out of a variety of materials, e.g., wooden blocks, string, or a blackboard. This demonstration is very effective when students see that the whole of human evolution equals an amount of time that can be represented by a single layer of tissue paper on a stack of blocks over a meter and a half tall. Measurements are also given for scales of 10 million years to the inch and 1 million years to the millimeter, which are useful for long strings or adding machine tape. In addition, instructions are given for creating a time scale using a variety of surfaces, e.g., a football field or the sidewalk in front of the school.

SCI LINKS.
*THE WORLD'S A CLICK AWAY*

Topic: Age of the Earth
Go to: www.scilinks.org
Code: AP010

## TEACHER'S NOTES:

The first exercise in this activity involves blocks. If the students cut the blocks themselves, then foam or Styrofoam would make good raw materials. Each student in the class can attempt this work, or one student can do it and the finished project can serve as demonstration. The idea is to construct a tower with the same width and depth but various size stories depending on the eras to be demonstrated. When the slices are stacked together they will give a three dimensional picture of the duration of geological time. We provide measurements for a tower 4 foot 7 inches tall. One foot equals one billion years, and 1 inch equals one billion years/12 or 83,000,000 years. The scale should be small enough so they can be handled readily, but large enough to give adequate representation to the shorter period of time. The scale used in this model satisfies both requirements. Students can get some math practice by inventing their own scales using the calculations included in this activity.

# The duration of time since Earth was formed

This activity provides several ways to demonstrate the great age of Earth. Earth is about 4.6 billion years old. How long a time span is this and for how much of this time have humans existed? One way to demonstrate these relationships is to make a tower out of wood or foam blocks to the "block" measurements in Table 5.1 below. Figure 5.1 shows a sketch of a 4 foot 7 inch tower spanning the history of the earth from its beginning in the year 4,600,000,000 BC, and showing thirteen major events.

Another good way to represent the great age of Earth is to make a string of time. Lay a string along a tape measure and tag important events at the appropriate points on the string, according to the second and third columns in the table below (10 million years to the inch or 1 million years to the millimeter.

An infinite number of devices are available to you to illustrate the duration of time in the context of the history of Earth (adding machine tape, a 24 hour clock, a football field, the sidewalk in front of your school, and so on.) You should not feel obliged to follow the method of the tower of blocks or the string. For example, let's say the hall in front of your classroom is 23 meters long. Divide the age of Earth (4,600,000,000 years) by 23 meters to give you a scale of 200,000,000 years per meter which is equal to 2 million years per centimeter or 200,000 years per millimeter. Now mark the important events in Table 5.1 according to this new scale. For example, the beginning of Earth (4.6 billion years) would be at "0". The oldest dated rock at 4 billion years ago would be at the 3-meter mark, because this occurred 600 million years after the origin of Earth and 1 meter equals 200 million years of time. The next significant date (the first evidence of life at 3.8 billion years ago) would be at the 4-meter mark.

# TABLE 5.1

Great moments in Earth history.
Values given for a tower of wood blocks calibrated at 1 foot to a billion years and a string of time calibrated to 10 million years to the inch and 1 million years to the millimeter.

| Blocks | 10my/inch | 1my/mm | Age and Events |
|---|---|---|---|
| 4'7" | 38'4" | 4,600mm | 4.6 billion years (by) or 4,600 million years (my): Origin of Earth. Asteroids and meteors coalesce into the proto-Earth, gradually adding to the mass of the planet. Meteorites generally yield dates of 4.6 by, since they are bits of debris floating around in space that never stuck to a planet. If you buy a meteorite at a rock shop and bring it to class, you can tell kids that they have touched the oldest thing in the entire solar system (see Chapter 3, Activity 1: Searching for Micrometeorites). |
| 4' | 33'4" | 4,000mm | 4.0 by: Oldest dated rock. |
| 3'10" | 31'8" | 3,800mm | 3.8 by: First evidence of life on Earth. This evidence is in the form of a chemical signature and not actual fossils, so there is some doubt about its validity. |
| 3'6" | 29'2" | 3,500mm | 3.5 by: First fossils. These are single-celled prokaryotes (bacteria) preserved in chert. |
| 8" | 5'5" | 650mm | 650 my: First animals. All soft-bodied (no skeletons). Some look like jellyfish or sea pens. |
| 6-1/2" | 4'6" | 545mm | 545 my: Beginning of the Cambrian Period and the Paleozoic Era. First shelled animals; trilobites, brachiopods, and others. |
| 5" | 3'6" | 425mm | 425 my: First land plants. |
| 4-1/2" | 3'2" | 380mm | 380 my: First land vertebrates (amphibians). |
| 3" | 2' | 245mm | 245 my: End of the Permian Period and Paleozoic Era and beginning of the Triassic Period and Mesozoic Era. Greatest extinction of the last 500 million years. About 96% of all species wiped out. |
| 2-1/2" | 1'9" | 210mm | 210 my: Beginning of the Jurassic Period. |
| 1-1/2" | 1'2" | 145mm | 145 my: Beginning of the Cretaceous Period. |
| 3/4" | 6 1/2" | 65mm | 65 my: Beginning of the Cenozoic Era and extinction of the dinosaurs. |
| Tissue paper width | 1/100" | 0.1mm | 100,000 yrs: Oldest modern human, Homo sapiens. |

FIGURE 5.1

Scale model of tower of blocks representing Earth history.

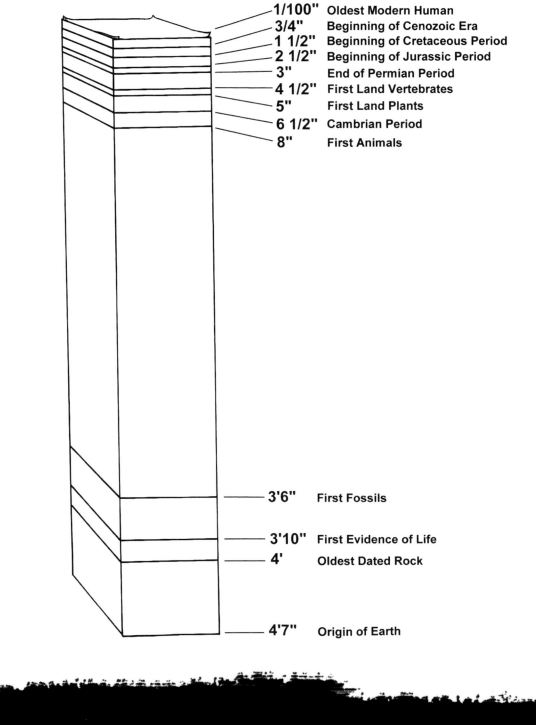

1/100"  Oldest Modern Human
3/4"  Beginning of Cenozoic Era
1 1/2"  Beginning of Cretaceous Period
2 1/2"  Beginning of Jurassic Period
3"  End of Permian Period
4 1/2"  First Land Vertebrates
5"  First Land Plants
6 1/2"  Cambrian Period
8"  First Animals

3'6"  First Fossils

3'10"  First Evidence of Life
4'  Oldest Dated Rock

4'7"  Origin of Earth

# How Did Dinosaurs Evolve?

In this chapter we present activities that address the methods of tracing evolution in fossils and give examples of two well-documented evolutionary transitions in dinosaurs. Activity 1 (*Archaeopteryx, Compsognathus,* and *Gallus domesticus*) investigates the many features that are shared by nonavian dinosaurs and birds. *Archaeopteryx* is one of the best examples of a "transitional" evolutionary form and this activity helps students realize that birds are actually feathered dinosaurs. Activity 2 (Homology) investigates the fact that all land-dwelling vertebrates have the same basic skeletal plan (backbone with vertebrae, four limbs with similar bone configurations, etc.) and that evolution has acted on these elements to produce specific adaptations for flying, running, climbing, swimming, etc. Discovering that you can find a homologous bone for your finger in a bat, whale and horse is a tremendous insight. Activity 3 (The method of cladistics) examines how we use specific characteristics of skeletons to create hypotheses of evolutionary relationships. This method allows scientists or students to generate hypotheses of evolutionary trees that can be tested by adding more specific characteristics. Activity 4 (Rates of evolution of Ceratopsia and contemporary reptiles) uses evolutionary trees to compare how rapidly ceratopsian dinosaurs (relatives of *Triceratops*) and modern reptiles have evolved.

Topic: Fossil Record
Go to: www.scilinks.org
Code: AP011

# Archaeopteryx, Compsognathus, and Gallus domesticus

FIGURE 6.1

Nested diagram showing similarities between a theropod (top), *Archeopteryx* (middle), and a chicken (*Gallus domesticus*) (bottom).

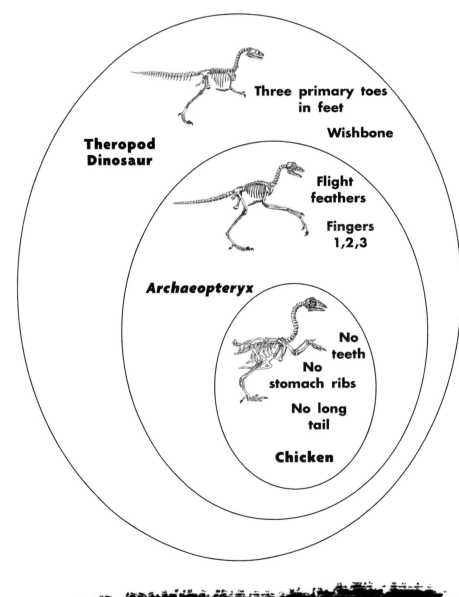

**Theropod Dinosaur**

**Three primary toes in feet**

**Wishbone**

*Archaeopteryx*

**Flight feathers**

**Fingers 1,2,3**

**Chicken**

**No teeth**

**No stomach ribs**

**No long tail**

*Archaeopteryx lithographica* is the geologically oldest known bird discovered. The fossil, about 150 million years old, was found in a limestone quarry in Solnhofen, Bavaria. In 1861, a print of a fossil feather was found in the limestone. The feather was a flight feather, shaped with its central vein off-center, characteristic of today's bird flight feathers. The following year, a skeleton of a fossil animal complete with feathers for flight was found in the same quarry. Since that time, seven more skeleton specimens have been found in the Solnhofen limestone. The skeletons of these eight fossils have been thoroughly studied by specialists who addressed the questions of habitat, biology, anatomical issues, the phylogenetic significance, and the evolution of flight of *Archaeopteryx*. They have published a vast array of scientific articles on the subject. By no means do they agree on every topic. But they do recognize that *Archaeopteryx* is a bird (primitive) and that it could fly.

Let's look at *Archaeopteryx* and compare it with its relative the

**SCiLINKS.**
*THE WORLD'S A CLICK AWAY*

Topic: Evolution in the Science Classroom

Go to: www.scilinks.org
Code: AP012

## FIGURE 6.2

Evolution of dinosaur to birds

modern bird, a chicken (*Gallus domesticus*), and with a presumed dinosaur-relative, *Compsognathus* (Figure 6.1). We will compare the three animals as skeletons because that is the only form the remains of the 150-million-years-old *Archaeopteryx* and *Compsognathus* occur. Each skeleton is in a circle that includes the characteristics of the animal. Each smaller enclosed circle represents the additional characteristics that set that animal apart from its ancestor. Therefore *Archaeopteryx* has flight feathers in addition to three primary toes in the feet and a wishbone. Find other traits that distinguish *Archaeopteryx* from its dinosaur ancestor and the chicken from *Archaeopteryx* (There are more than those listed.).

The intermediate position of *Archaeopteryx* between the modern bird and the nonavian dinosaur is fairly obvious in the

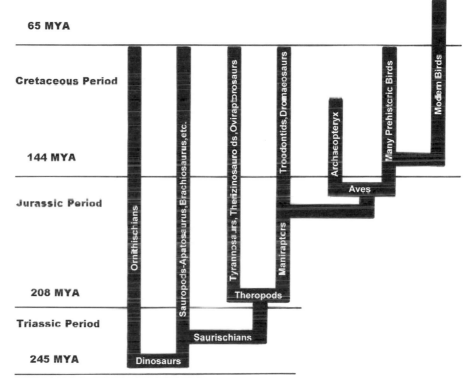

characteristics it shares with each. *Archaeopteryx* is about as much a half dinosaur and a half bird as one could find. Yet it clearly represents a missing link between the bird and the dinosaur. As such it occupies the position in the evolutionary boundary between the thousands of species of living birds and extinct dinosaurs. The evolution of dinosaurs and birds can be viewed in Figure 6.2.

The discovery of one species of fossil can suggest a major shift in the thinking about the course evolution has taken. But the appearance of *Archaeopteryx* has raised far more questions about the origin of bird flight than it has answered. What was the origin of birds? What is the ancestry of *Archaeopteryx*? How did bird flight evolve? Could *Archaeopteryx* fly? And how? From the ground or from the tree? How well? Could it perch in a tree using its hallux? What was its diet?

Then there was the question concerning what *Archaeopteryx* looked like when it was alive. Its restoration when shown with *Compsognathus* takes a bit of creative imagination, as in the illustration of the animal by the shore of the Tethys Sea about 150 million years ago (Figure 6.3). You can see that though their skeletons were quite similar, their bodies appeared to be different. How much of the difference was the addition of feathers to the body cover?

FIGURE 6.3

*Archaeopteryx* and *Compsognathus* 150 mya at Solnhofen

# Homology

Ever since vertebrates crawled out of the sea, they had a similarity of body structure resulting from a commonality of ancestry known as homology. Such signs of evolution are called homologous structures. The bones of the forelimbs of vertebrates are constructed from the same skeletal elements in all vertebrates, from the coelacanth fish to modern man. The basic architecture is seen in the makeup of all vertebrates

Topic: Vertebrate Evolution
Go to: www.scilinks.org
Code: AP011

## FIGURE 6.4

Bones in the forelimbs of vertebrate animals.

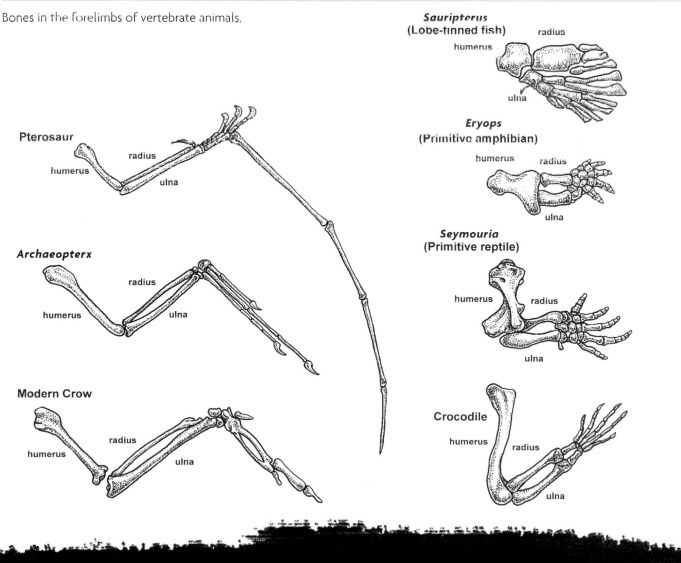

### FIGURE 6.5

The embryos of a chicken (left) and a human (right).

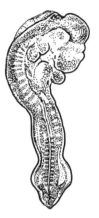
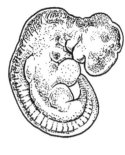

from emerging fish, amphibians, reptiles, sea lizards, crocodiles, pterosaurs, dinosaurs, birds, and mammals (Figure 6.4). The bones of the forelimbs are scapula, humerus, radius, ulna, carpals, metacarpals, and phalanges. Each animal has the same general architecture but the forelimbs are modified for different functions depending on the needs of the animal. These functions may include running, walking, climbing, flying, swimming, seizing food, and mating. Skeletal specializations lead to the survival of different species of animals.

All organs in the vertebrate body have homologous structures that have been modified by evolution, causing changes in the bodies to adapt to different environmental factors. The skin, kidneys, vascular system, and digestive system of all animals are constantly changing as the animals adapt to changing environments. We know that anatomical structures have changed dramatically from their earlier forms, but we have no clear evidence. The fossils of most species have not been preserved. We can infer changes by observing embryos, or

### FIGURE 6.6

Crests on the heads of duckbill dinosaurs.

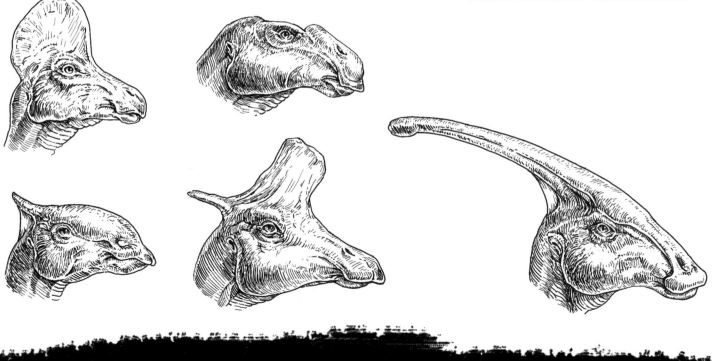

## FIGURE 6.7

Forelimbs of *Deinonychus*, *Struthiomimus*, *Triceratops*, and *Tyrannosaurus*.

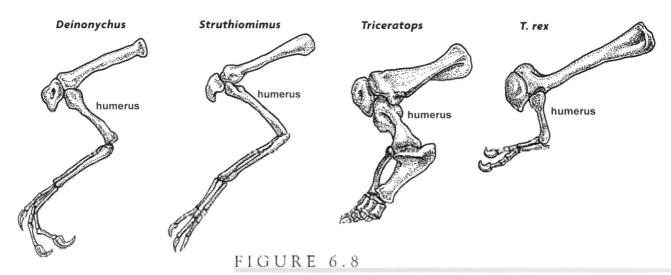

## FIGURE 6.8

A human and *Brachiosaurus*.

we can see organs that have become vestigial. Or we can infer what the kidney was like in a fish or in an amphibian, but we don't have the clear fossil proof we get from the hard fossil bones that endure millions of years in the crust of Earth. Bones are the most durable and revealing fossil evidence. Nevertheless, embryos suggest much of the evolutionary history of vertebrates. Compare the embryo of the chicken with the embryo of the human (Figure 6.5).

In both the embryos, note gill pouches and the post anal tail. In each embryo, the homologous pouches will develop into structures other than gill pouches (though in fish and amphibians they will develop into gill pouches). The tails of fish and most vertebrates develop prominent external tails, but in most birds and apes, the tail is not an external structure, even though the embryo has a prominent tail. Homologous structures become modified or disappear during the embryological development of the animal.

Let's take the dinosaurs for example. For over 200 million years they adapted to conditions from pole to pole, from mountains, to deserts, and to jungles. In that interval, every force in nature acted upon them to produce a diversity of structure. For example, the crests of duckbill dinosaurs show a remarkable diversity that is probably related to display in order to attract mates (Figure 6.6)

The forelimbs of dinosaurs also became specialized for particular functions (Figure 6.7). The forelimbs of *Deinonychus* and *Struthiomimus* were slender and flexible for grasping, while those of *Triceratops* were thick and strong for supporting its great weight. There is some controversy surrounding the purpose of the forelimbs in *Tyrannosaurus*. Though they have claws and look like they might have been useful for grasping things, the arms were too short to reach the mouth! Can you think of what purpose they might have served?

Dinosaurs also varied tremendously in size. For example *Brachiosaurus*, the largest of the sauropod dinosaurs, weighed over 70 tons (Figure 6.8), while the skeleton of *Mussasaurus*, one of the smallest sauropods, fits in two human hands (Figure 6.9).

## FIGURE 6.9

Skeleton of juvenile *Mussasaurus.*

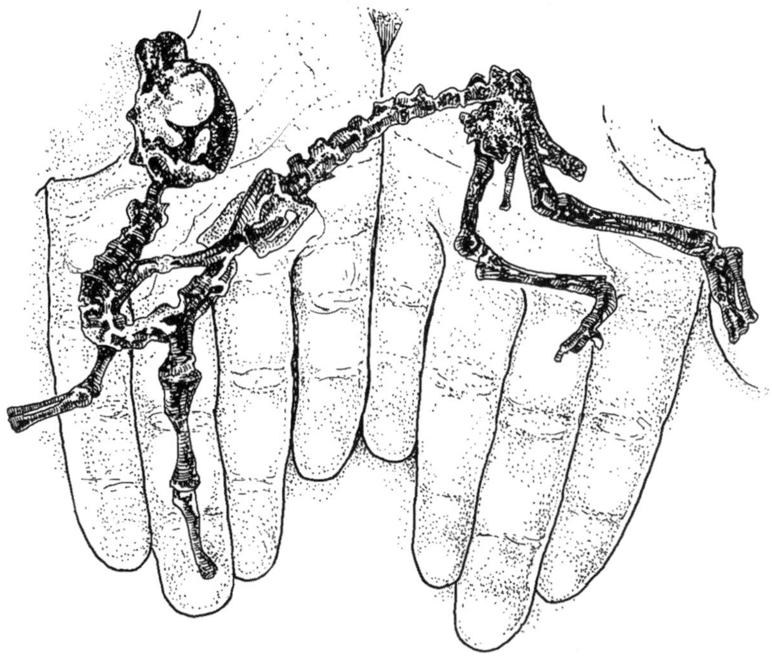

# The method of cladistics

In the 18th century, Carl von Linné invented a scheme for naming and classifying all forms of life on Earth. He gave each species a first name and a last name in a language that does not change—Latin or Greek. For example, *Tyrannosaurus rex* is the genus and species name of one type of dinosaur. It is the **binomial system of nomenclature,** where every kind of organism, living or extinct, has a unique name. In addition to the name, Linné invented a classification scheme in which the species is placed in more inclusive boxes within boxes. For example, *Tyrannosaurus rex* is placed in (family) Tyrannosauridae, (super family) Theropoda, (order) Saurischia, and (class) Dinosauria. Thus the Linnean system of classification was organized as a nested hierarchy.

Such an organization was thought to tell the course of evolution. Which species, and when this species evolved into a new species, became the thing to know. The Linnean system failed in this regard. Classification schemes grouped organisms on the basis of similarity of appearance rather than on the reliability of the shared ancestry. A German entomologist, Willi Hennig, invented a system of classification that would reflect the patterns of ancestry and that is used by most of biologist today. It is called **cladistics**—the branching order of common ancestry. The recency of common ancestry can be approximated by the distribution of characteristics of the organisms that are available. Cladistics is the method of searching for the simplest distribution of derived characteristics to approximate the historical branching of the Tree of Life.

Let's illustrate how cladistics works by comparing the characteristic of four carnivorous dinosaurs: *Allosaurus*, *Deinonychus*, *Albertosaurus*, and *Tyrannosaurus*.

SCI LINKS
THE WORLD'S A CLICK AWAY

Topic: Systems of Classification
Go to: www.scilinks.org
Code: AP011

|  | Allosaurus | Deinonychus | Albertosaurus | Tyrannosaurus |
|---|---|---|---|---|
| Hinge in lower jaw | Yes | Yes | Yes | Yes |
| Wishbone | Yes | Yes | Yes | Yes |
| Bipedal | Yes | Yes | Yes | Yes |
| Retractable sickle claw | No | Yes | No | No |
| Backward-pointing pubis | No | Yes | No | No |
| Number of fingers | 3 | 3 | 2 | 2 |
| Third metatarsal foot | Unpinched | Unpinched | Pinched | Pinched |
| Anklebone | Short | Tall | Tall | Tall |
| Tip of ischium | Expanded | Pointed | Pointed | Pointed |

We note that the four carnivorous dinosaurs share three common characteristics: a hinge in the middle of the lower jaw, a wishbone, and bipedal upright stance. These are some of their primitive characteristics that they share with their common ancestor. Two characteristics are unique in *Deinonychus*: a retractable claw and a backward-pointing pubis. These two features must have appeared after the ancestor of *Deinonychus* evolved from the other three. Then there are four derived characteristics that arose somewhere in the course of time.

So let us now draw a "cladogram" for the four carnivorous dinosaurs, keeping in mind that the best hypothesis is the one with the fewest number of evolutionary changes (Figure 6.10).

Traits 1, 2, and 3 are primitive traits common to each of the four animals. At juncture "c," *Allosaurus* branches off and the remaining three continue. Then the anklebone becomes tall and the tip of the ischium becomes pointed in all of the remaining three animals. At point "b" *Deinonychus* branches out and the animals derive retractable sickle claws and a backward-pointing pubis. The remaining animals continue to change by developing two fingers instead of three, and a pinched third metatarsal in the foot. At point "a" *Albertosaurus* branches off, and *Tyrannosaurus* continues on. This is the best hypothesis with the data at hand. But more data can come from new discoveries of fossils and additional characteristics.

### FIGURE 6.10

Cladogram for *Allosaurus*, *Deinonychus*, *Albertosaurus*, and *Tyrannosaurus*.

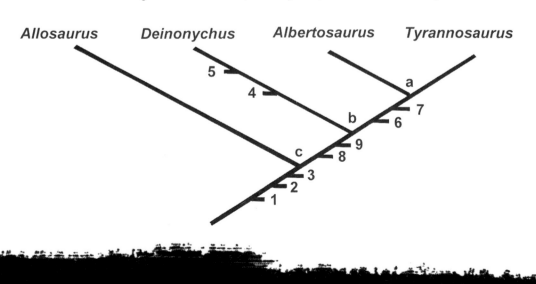

# FIGURE 6.11

A cladogram showing the position of the dinosaur among the four-limbed vertebrates.

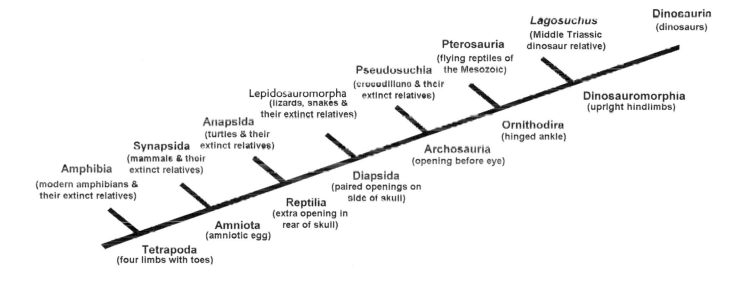

The questions below refer to Figure 6.11.

1. Which is the first vertebrate to appear on land? What is its distinctive feature? Name one living animal example.
2. What animal group developed an amniotic egg? How many of the seven animal groups produce an amniotic egg? Which animal did not produce an amniotic egg?
3. How do the skulls of Anapsida (tortoises and turtles), Lepidosauromorpha (lizards and snakes), and Pseudosuchia (crocodile) differ from one another? If you had a skull of each, how would tell them apart?
4. The hinged ankle is an added characteristic of the Tetrapoda, the Amniote, the Reptilia, the Diapsida and the Archosauria. But these animals still do not stand upright on their hind legs. What is the genetic trait that makes this possible and characterizes a new and successful species?
5. According to this scheme of classification, who are your closest relatives from among the seven units of classification. Does this surprise you?

FIGURE 6.12

A basic cladogram of the relationships among the major groups of dinosaurs.

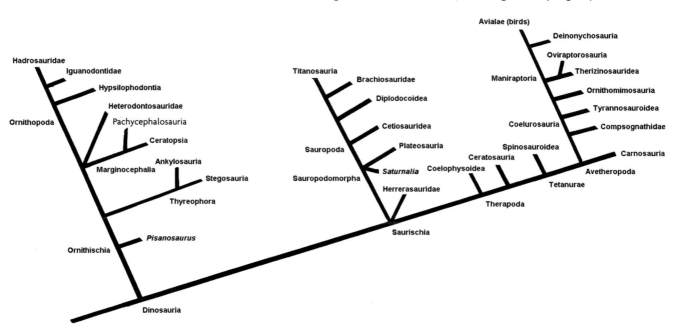

The questions below refer to Figure 6.12.

1. The first branching of the dinosaurs leads to the order Ornithischia. The first one is Pisanosaurus, and the last one before the extinction of the dinosaurs is _____. The special traits of this family were found to have an advanced social system with extended care of the offspring. What did each species eat?

2. The second branching produced the order Saurischia all "lizard-hipped" dinosaurs. They produced the giant Sauropod, which grew larger and larger. Diplodocidae, Brachiosauridae, and Titanosauria were the familiar animals that achieved a highly social life producing eggs, childcare, and family units. How do you account for the increasing care given to offspring by the parents?

3. We then come to the suborder Theropoda, which are the "bird-footed" carnivorous dinosaurs. The third branch, turning to the left, is the family Compsognathidae, a small Saurischian dinosaur and including many of the small raptors. Many of these dinosaurs are found with feathers. And some of the feathered dinosaurs (birds) could fly. When all the dinosaurs became extinct, the birds took over. Can you imagine a bird as a kind of dinosaur?

4. This section of the cladogram put Deinonychosauria farther out than the position of the family of Tyrannosauroidea. In fact, there is a great distance between the two. In figure 6.10 their position is reversed, with Deinonchosauria with sickle claws, the third metatarsal tarsal unpinched, three fingers and backward pointing pubis. How do you explain this?

5. *Archaeopteryx*, the famous bird found in Jurassic rock formation, was discovered in rock along with fossils of the dinosaur *Compsognathus*, a small bird-like creature whose skeleton was mistaken for *Archaeopteryx*. In fact, some early paleontologists were not able to distinguish their skeletons when the fossil of *Archaeopteryx* did not show an imprint of their feathers. What do you consider the significance of this fact?

Holtz, T.R., Jr. 2002. Chasing *Tyrannosaurus* and *Deinonychus* around the tree of life: Classifying dinosaurs. In *Dinosaurs: The science behind the stories*, eds. J. G. Scotchmoor, D. A. Springer, B. H. Breithaupt, and A. F. Fiorillo, 31–38. Alexandria: American Geological Institute.

# Rates of evolution of Ceratopsia and contemporary reptiles

FIGURE 6.13

Reconstructions of *Psittacosaurus* (top), *Protoceratops* (middle), and *Ceratopsid* (bottom).

An important part of the final chapter of dinosaur history involved large Ceratopsia that measured from five to nine meters in length and weighed up to four tons. They were equipped with some arrangement of sharp horn on the brow or snout, and a large body shield of bone covering the neck of the animal that protected the skull. These were the Ceratopsia that may have protected themselves by the aggressive action of ramming and stabbing the predators of the Cretaceous Period, in contrast to the animal's cousins ankylosaurs, stegosaurs, and hadrosaurs, which were relatively passive to the attackers (Bakker 1982).

The Ceratopsia originated in Asia (Mongolia) during the early Cretaceous Period. Fossil remains of small bipedal *Psittacosaurus* must be close to the origin (Figure 6.13). They had a parrot-shaped beak and the beginning of a neck shield. In the same region of Mongolia, a small *Protoceratops*, dating from later in the Cretaceous Period, was discovered by Roy Chapman Andrew in 1922 (Figure 6.13). With it was found the first egg nest anywhere on Earth. Curiously, the suborder Ceratopsia is only known to exist in Mongolia and mainly in a strip of land running south from Alberta and British Columbia through the western United States. In North America they were here for only about 15 million years, but in that time there were many species and genera. The most famous were *Triceratops*, the last and the most abundant species of the line (Figure 6.13). Besides its horn and shield, one of the additional reasons for its success were its teeth—40-centimeter long batteries set in jaws behind its parrot beak, shearing rather than grinding teeth, with cutting edges for slicing up tough fibrous plant material. Another trait of the

Ceratopsia was their forward speed powered by strong leg muscles. With its head down it could drive its horns into the belly of a menacing *Tyrannosaurus*.

In the 15 million years the Ceratopsia lived in North America, they were a rapidly evolving suborder. There were at least seven genera and several dozen species, with each genus going extinct about each 5 million years. That is an extremely fast rate of evolution. The one characteristic that appeared to dominate the body of the Ceratopsia in the closing moments of the Cretaceous Period were the horns and the ramming speed of the body. (Others contend the horns were a sexual selection trait.) *Triceratops* made up 80% of the horned dinosaurs at the close of the Cretaceous Period.

About 80 million years ago, there were at least three genera of Ceratopsia and possibly 5 species of each one. About 75 to 70 mya there were at least two genera of Ceratopsia and about 5 species of each. Then about 70 to 65 mya, there were at least two genera and about 5 species of each one. About 65 million years ago, all of the Ceratopsia, and the entire remaining dinosaurs, became extinct. Even the *Triceratops* with its *Tyrannosaurus* killing horns, its neck-shield, its two-ton body powered by muscular legs, and beak and teeth that rendered tree trunks into granular meal, could not survive the ultimate extinction of the dinosaurs.

Everyone wonders why the dinosaurs did not survive. Why did the crocodile, the turtle, and the clam survive instead? These acquired food, withstood adverse weather and climate, and predators and airborne toxins did not molest them. One difference between the dinosaurs and the crocodiles and the turtles was that the Ceratopsia was changing genera every 5 million years and the other was changing genera every 35 millions years.

SCI**LINKS**.
**THE WORLD'S A CLICK AWAY**

Topic: Evolution and Adaptation
Go to: www.scilinks.org
Code: AP015

# Diversity, Classification, and Taxonomy

This chapter analyzes how diversity is measured, how dinosaurs are classified, and their distribution in time and space. Activity 1 (The ages of the reptiles, the archosaurs [dinosaurs, pterosaurs and crocodiles], and the therapsids [mammals]) describes the traditional classification of dinosaurs and places the major groups in a time framework. The activity concludes with a matching exercise that reveals the descriptive roots of dinosaur names. Activity 2 (How big was *Ultrasaurus macIntosh*?) looks at the taxonomy of what may have been the biggest dinosaur ever and invites students to analyze the major feature that distinguishes it from its relatives: size. Activity 3 (The worldwide distribution of dinosaurs) shows where in the world dinosaurs have been found and the ages of these dinosaur-bearing deposits. It then invites the students to compare the locations of their hometowns with the location of dinosaur deposits. Activity 4 (Measuring diversity) defines exactly what is meant by "diversity" and the different ways it can be measured. Surprisingly, the concept of diversity includes both the number of species and the abundance of each species. This activity emphasizes higher-level math skills to calculate diversities for different hypothetical scenarios.

Topic: Classification
Go to: www.scilinks.org
Code: AP016

Topic: Taxonomy
Go to: www.scilinks.org
Code: AP017

# The ages of the reptiles, the archosaurs (dinosaurs, pterosaurs and crocodiles), and the therapsids (mammals)

Beginning during the Permian Period, we see the reptiles coming into prominence and becoming the dominant vertebrate present. Along with the therapsids (mammals), they make their appearance during the Permian and become the dominant fauna during the Triassic Period. During the Jurassic and Cretaceous Periods another group, the dinosaurs,

## FIGURE 7.1

Diagram showing the terrestrial ecological niches dominated by the Archosauria.

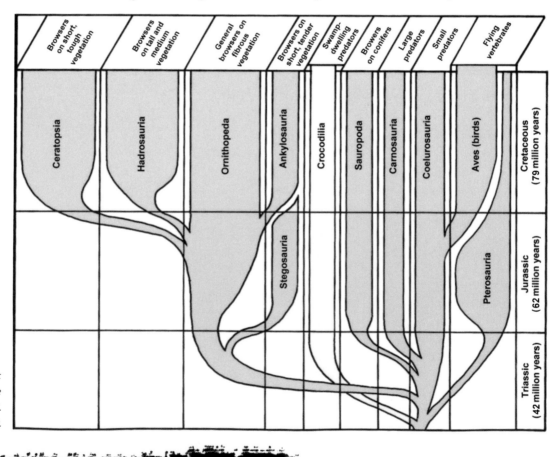

Adapted from *Archosauria:
A New Look at the
Old Dinosaur*, by J. C.
McLoughlin. Viking, 1979.

# FIGURE 7.2

Relative proportions of Reptiles, Therapsids/Mammals, and Archosaurs through time.

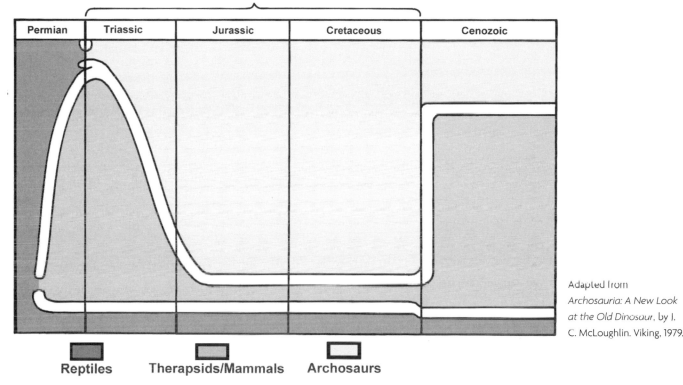

Adapted from
*Archosauria: A New Look
at the Old Dinosaur*, by J.
C. McLoughlin. Viking, 1979.

then replaced the therapsids as the dominant group of animals. The group of dinosaurs evolved from the reptiles in the early Triassic Period and forced the reptiles to a lesser role in life. Dinosaurs then dominated Earth for about 170 million years. Then something happened rather suddenly about 65 million years ago. The dinosaurs and pterosaurs disappeared, except for the crocodiles and the birds. The Cenozoic Era brought the mammal back as the dominant animal in the Age of Mammals. This relationship is illustrated in Figure 7.1.

As the Triassic Period opened the reptiles diversified into the crocodiles, the pterosaurs, and the dinosaurs (Figure 7.2). It started with the crocodiles, with three orders: the Protosuchia, the Mesosuchia, and the Eusuchia; the Pterosauria, with two orders: Rhamphorynchoidea and the Pterodactyloidea; the Dinosauria with five orders of bird-hipped (Ornithischia): the Ceratopsia, the Hadrosauria, the Ornithopoda, the Stegosauria, and the Ankylosauria; and the Dinosauria with three orders of lizard-hipped (Saurischia): the Sauropoda, the Carnosauria, and the Coelurosauria; and the birds of the class Aves.

At about the 65-million-year mark the living dinosaurs and their Archosauria relative, the Pterosauria, became extinct (Figure 7.2). Only the birds and the

TABLE 7.1

Taxonomic hierarchy of the dinosaurs

| | | |
|---|---|---|
| Kingdom | Animalia | |
| Phylum | Chordata | |
| Class | Reptilia | |
| Class | Synapsida | |
| Order | Pelycosauria (Dimetridon) | |
| Order | Therapsida (Cynognathus) | |
| Class | Archaesauria | |
| Sub Class | Ornithischia | |
| Order | Hadrosauria | |
| Order | Ornithopoda | |
| Order | Ankylosauria | |
| Order | Stegosauria | |
| Sub Class | Saurischia | |
| Order | Sauropoda | |
| Order | Carnosauria | |
| Order | Coelurosauria | |
| Order\Class | Aves | |
| Order | Pterosauria | |
| Order | Crocodilia | |
| Family | (such as) Hadrosauridae and Stegosauridae | |
| Genus and Species (such as) *Parasaurolophus walkeri* | | |

crocodiles survived. The crocodiles and the birds survived possibly because their terrestrial niche was water and air. At the beginning of the Cenozoic Era, about 65 million years ago, the land habitats were devoid of large vertebrates, but not for long. The mammals (the Therapsida of the Permian Period and early Mesozoic Era) soon exploded on Earth into about every environmental niche. We quickly shifted from the Age of the Dinosaurs on land and the Age of Pterosaurs in the air to the Age of Mammals on land and the Age of Birds in the air. So today we have a few reptiles (snakes, lizards, and turtles), a few crocodiles, and several hundred thousand species of birds and mammals adapted to the land, sea, and air.

This is a matching exercise in which you are to match the name of the dinosaur with its translation. Taxonomists use Latin or Greek in scientific names of organisms. Latin and ancient Greek are dead languages and the vocabulary will not change with time. Scientists across the globe use the same dead language to name organisms. A language genius can get seven or more correct without help from reference books. Write the correct corresponding letter in the space next to the number.

_____ 1. Protoceratops
_____ 2. Triceratops
_____ 3. Styrcosaurus
_____ 4. Monoclonius
_____ 5. Ceratopsia
_____ 6. Allosaurus
_____ 7. Tyrannosaurus
_____ 8. Diplodocus
_____ 9. Brachiosaurus
_____ 10. Brontosaurus
_____ 11. Hypsilophodon
_____ 12. Archaeopteryx
_____ 13. Compsognathus
_____ 14. Ceolophysis
_____ 15. Ornithischia
_____ 16. Ornithopoda
_____ 17. Ornithosuchus
_____ 18. Saurornithoides
_____ 19. Seymouria
_____ 20. Struthiomimus
_____ 21. Ankylosaurus
_____ 22. Kentrosaurus
_____ 23. Stegosaurus
_____ 24. Psittacosaurus
_____ 25. Saltopus
_____ 26. Pachycephalosaurus
_____ 27. Gorgosaurs
_____ 28. Hadrosaurus
_____ 29. Plateosaurus
_____ 30. Parasaurolophus
_____ 31. Longisquamata
_____ 32. Comptosaurus
_____ 33. Iguanodon

a. weird lizard
b. stiffened lizard
c. old wing
d. armed lizard
e. chambered lizard
f. flexible lizard
g. dragging lizard
h. horned lizard
i. hollow boned
j. elegant jawed
k. double beamed
l. horrible lizard
m. big lizard
n. high crested tooth
o. iguano tooth
p. pointed lizard
q. long scale
r. one horned
s. bird hips
t. bird feet
u. tyrant lizard
w. thick headed
x. sort of crested
y. bird feet
z. parrot lizard
aa. flat lizard
bb. bird crocodile
cc. early horned face
dd. leaping foot
ee. lizard-like bird
ff. plated lizard
gg. three horned lizard
hh. ostrich mimic

# How big was *Ultrasaurus macIntosh*?

SCI**LINKS**®
*THE WORLD'S A CLICK AWAY*

Topic: Comparing Dinosaurs
Go to: www.scilinks.org
Code: AP018

James Jensen of Brigham Young University uncovered two giant sauropods in 1972 and 1979 in Colorado. In 1972 he found one dinosaur that he recognized was an enlarged form of *Diplodocus*, which he named *Supersaurus*. But then in 1979 he discovered a larger member of the Brachiosauridae family, a giant of an animal that made the others seem small. He named it *Ultrasaurus macIntosh* in 1985. The taxonomy of the species is

## FIGURE 7.3

Drawing of the skeleton of *Brachiosaurus* on display in the Humboldt Museum in Berlin, Germany (right), and a drawing of the forelimb and scapula from *Ultrasaurus* (left).

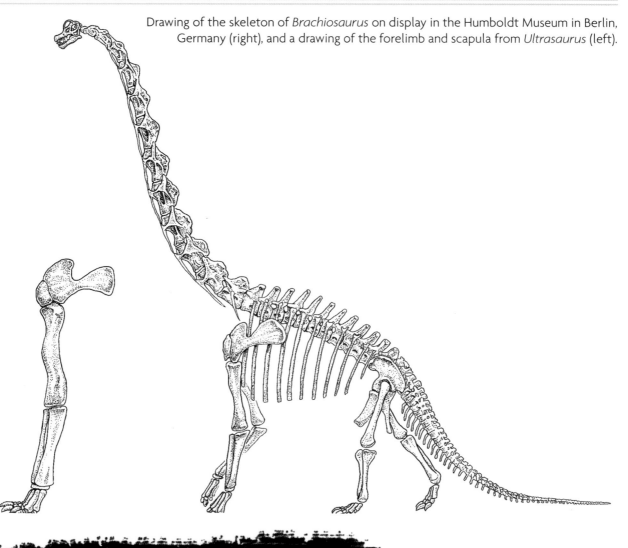

## FIGURE 7.4

Reconstruction of *Brachiosaurus*.

**Class:** Dinosauria
**Subclass:** Sauropodomorpha
**Order:** Sauropoda
**Suborder:** Titanosauria
**Family:** Brachiosauridae
**Genus:** *Ultrasaurus*
**Species:** *macIntosh*
**Period:** Late Jurassic
**Age:** Kimmeridgian-Tithonian 144–156 MYA
**Body Parts Found:** Dorsal Vertebrae and a shoulder blade

Sauropods fed by stripping the leaves of evergreen trees. Presumably the sauropods grew taller as the trees grew. The front legs of sauropods grew longer than the hind legs to support the longer and heavier neck that reached upwards. The body sloped downward to the smaller legs and the tail of the animals. The neck of the animal rose like a crane and was supported by many cables and lightweight vertebrae. The head of the sauropod was small, consisting of a mouth with peg-like teeth adapted for stripping 500–1,000 pounds of leaves a day. The nostrils were on the roof of the skull, presumably to allow the animal to eat and breathe without interference. They traveled in a herd and probably knew few enemies, although when they died their bodies were an obvious feast for the carnivores. Since few eggs have ever been found, some paleontologists think that sauropods may have given live birth to their young.

The largest assembled *Brachiosaurus* in the world is in the Humboldt Museum in Germany. It is 39 feet tall at the shoulder. It is 74 feet long from head to tail. And it is estimated to have weighed 77 tons!

James Jensen has estimated *Ultrasaurus macIntosh* to be 1/3 larger than *Brachiosaurus*; that would be 60 feet tall at the shoulder, 98 feet long from head to tail, and a weight of 135 tons.

Figure 7.3 shows a mounted skeleton of the *Brachiosaurus* from Tendaguru, Tanzania, Africa. Beside this skeleton is the left front leg of *Ultrasaurus macIntosh* from the feet to the scapula, a total height of 60 feet. Compare the leg of each animal to get a sense of the difference in size. Figure 7.4 illustrates what the *Brachiosaurus* may have looked like in the flesh.

Your task is to draw, sculpt, or sketch *Brachiosaurus* and *Ultrasaurus* together, showing their differences in size as they stand in the Jurassic forest.

# The worldwide distribution of dinosaurs

Dinosaurs first appeared on Earth about 235 million years ago, during the Late Triassic Period. During their first 30 million years, they produced a diversity of species that spread around the world. Then for the next 140 million years, the planet was theirs to exploit worldwide.

From the Antarctic Circle in the south to the Arctic Circle in the north, the dinosaurs adapted to the different climates of Earth. They adapted to the hot, dry deserts and to the dense forest. Where they lived, they left behind their fossil skeletons, their preserved skin, footprints, eggs, and excrement. The study of the distribution in space and time is the science of **paleobiogeography.** In this field the three items that must be known when a dinosaur is discovered are:

1. The precise geographical location,
2. the age of the rock in which it found, and
3. which dinosaur species remains are represented.

Table 7.2 describes the global distribution of dinosaurs during their 170-million-year reign as the dominant class of animal on Earth. It starts with the appearance of dinosaurs in the late Triassic and follows the reign to the end of the late Cretaceous when, approximately 65 million years ago, the dinosaurs suddenly became extinct. In all, there are six time intervals, and each one recounts where dinosaurs have been found by continent, country, or state, from Antarctica to the Arctic Circle. If dinosaurs were thought to have lived all over the world, why are there so many blank spaces—geographic locations where there are no records of dinosaurs? China was covered with dinosaurs from about 235 million years ago until they went extinct, while in other countries, fossil sites are spotty or are not known at all.

Why does the distribution of dinosaur fossils across Earth appear so random and spotty? A few of the major reasons are:

1. Many sites have not been explored by paleontologists. They are dangerous or inhospitable, the rocks are far underground, or the fossiliferous deposits have washed away. About 75% of the known dinosaurs have been found in Argentina, Canada, China, England, Mongolia, and United States.
2. Rock of the correct age was not preserved or is not exposed. Middle Jurassic rock is rare as an outcrop. Some ancient environments fail to support fossilization. For example, upland environments such as mountains erode away before fossils can form.

During their 170 million years living on this planet, and in the many diverse climates, dinosaurs changed a considerable amount to adapt to the environments. The Sauropoda

## TABLE 7.2.

Global Dinosaur Distribution

| Era | Geographic Locale | Countries where dinosaurs lived |
|---|---|---|
| Late Triassic (235–208 mya) | North America | Canada (Northwest Territories, Nova Scotia); United States (Arizona, Colorado, Massachusetts, New Jersey, New Mexico, New York, North Carolina, Pennsylvania, Utah) |
| | Europe | Belgium, England, France, Germany, Italy, Scotland, Switzerland, Wales |
| | Greater Asia | China, India |
| | South America | Brazil, Argentina |
| | Africa | Lesotho, Madagascar, Morocco, South Africa |
| | Australasia | Australia |
| Early Jurassic (208–178 mya) | North America | Canada (Nova Scotia); United States (Arizona, Colorado, Connecticut, Massachusetts, New Jersey, Utah, Wyoming); Mexico |
| | Europe | England, France, Germany, Hungary, Portugal, Sweden |
| | Greater Asia | China, India, Iran |
| | South America | Brazil, Venezuela |
| | Africa | Algeria, Lesotho, Morocco, Namibia, South Africa, Zimbabwe |
| | Antarctica | trans-Antarctic Mountains |
| Middle Jurassic (178–157 mya) | Europe | England, France, Portugal, Scotland |
| | Greater Asia | China |
| | South America | Argentina, Chile |
| | Africa | Morocco, Algeria |
| | Australasia | Australia |
| Late Jurassic (157–145 mya) | North America | United States (Alaska, Colorado, Montana, Oklahoma, New Mexico, South Dakota, Texas, Utah, Wyoming) |
| | Europe | England, France, Germany, Portugal, Spain, Switzerland |
| | Greater Asia | China, India, Thailand |
| | South America | Argentina, Chile, Columbia |
| | Africa | Madagascar, Malawi, Morocco, Niger, South Africa, Tanzania, Zimbabwe |
| | Australasia | New Zealand |
| Early Cretaceous (145–97 mya) | North America | Canada (British Colombia); United States (Alaska, Arkansas, Arizona, Colorado, Idaho, Kansas, Maryland, Montana, Nebraska, New Mexico, Oklahoma, South Dakota, Texas, Utah, Wyoming) |
| | Europe | Belgium, Croatia, England, France, Germany, Italy, Norway, Portugal, Romania, Spain |
| | Greater Asia | China, Georgia, Japan, Kazakhstan, Mongolia, South Korea, Thailand |
| | South America | Argentina, Brazil, Chile |
| | Africa | Algeria, Cameroon, Libya, Malawi, Mali, Morocco, Mozambique, Niger, Sudan, South Africa, Tunisia, Zambia, Zimbabwe |
| | Australasia | Australia |
| Late Cretaceous (97–65 mya) | North America | Canada (Alberta, British Colombia, Northwest Territories, Saskatchewan, Yukon Territory); Honduras, Mexico, United States (Alabama, Alaska, Arizona, California, Colorado, Delaware, Georgia, Kansas, Maryland, Mississippi, Missouri, Montana, Nevada, New Jersey, New Mexico, North Carolina, North Dakota, Oregon, South Dakota, Texas, Utah, Wyoming) |
| | Europe | Austria, Belgium, Czech Republic, England, France, Netherlands, Portugal, Romania, Russia, Spain, Ukraine |
| | Greater Asia | China, India, Israel, Japan, Kazakhstan, Laos, Mongolia, Russia, Syria, Tajikistan, Uzbekistan |
| | South America | Argentina, Bolivia, Brazil, Chile, Colombia, Peru, Uruguay |
| | Africa | Algeria, Egypt, Kenya, Madagascar, Morocco, Niger, South Africa |
| | Australasia | New Zealand |
| | Antarctica | Antarctic peninsula |

that occupied the open plains of central Canada and United States were enormous animals, but fossils of the same animal found in what is today Romania (then an island in Europe) were small, an illustration of Island Dwarfism. In Australia, when it was farther south than it is today, it presented a cool climate to its dinosaurs, at 70 to 85 degrees south latitude. As a result, these dinosaurs were much smaller then the ones that lived in more temperate regions. But that is only part of the story. At the Antarctic Circle the daylight is very long during the austral summer and very short during the austral winter. The dinosaur Leaellynasaur's brain was covered with a very large optic lobe. This suggested it may have evolved a heightened sense of vision during the extended darkness of the polar winter.

Of even more significance, over their 170 million years of life on Earth, the dinosaurs developed a social life that including caring for young and maintaining protection for the entire tribe.

You can begin your study paleobiogeography by referring to Table 7.2 (page 97).

1. First note which states have rock close to the surface of the ground that contain dinosaur fossils.
2. Which states are near where you live? If you have none close, obtain a map of rock formations for your state. Look for Late Triassic; Early, Middle, and Late Jurassic; and Early and Late Cretaceous.
3. Describe where rock formation from each period is located relative to the others.
4. Describe the thickness of the rocks from each period (the total depth of all six of the period-specific rock formations).
5. If there is no Triassic to Cretaceous rock in your state, find out what happened to it. If you live in Hawaii, the land did not exist then. But how about Florida and Ohio? Is it possible that the record for 170 million years of dinosaurs fossils could have been washed away into the sea?
6. What could be done to look for fossils that lie well beneath the rock surface?

Maps can be obtained from the geological survey office in your state, your librarian may help find some, the internet is a good source, or ask your geology teacher.

Forster, C. 2002. Where dinosaurs roamed the Earth. In *Dinosaurs: The science behind the stories*, eds. J. G. Scotchmoor, D. A. Springer, B. H. Breithaupt, and A. F. Fiorillo, pp. 45–52. Alexandria: American Geological Institute.

# Measuring diversity

We have heard a lot about the global biodiversity crisis and the loss of countless species. What is diversity? How is it measured? How do you determine the diversity of an environment like a rain forest or a marine bay? The most obvious measure is simply the number of species present in an environment. This is called species richness. The species richness of a sample would be the number of species present in that sample.

How do you measure the diversity of an environment? If the environment is large, like a rain forest, you can't actually go and count all the species because it would take too long (besides, the animals wouldn't hold still!). So scientists take a sample that they hope will be representative of the community. You might do this by counting all species within a 10 square foot area or counting all the species that you encountered as you walked a straight line from one end of the environment to the other. Obviously a sample will not include all the species in the environment because many species are rare and present in only a few locations, or present only during certain times of the year (such as migratory birds).

## The effect of sample size on your measure of diversity

If you want to determine the species richness of a forest and choose a small sample size, say all of the species within a one square foot area, you will not find as many species in that sample as you would if you chose a larger sample, such as a ten square foot area. The larger the sample you take, the more species you will find. Try this experiment in your class.

Get sheets of paper representing as many different colors as you can (or any colored object of a uniform size will do, such as colored beads). Cut each sheet into small squares about 3/4 inch on a side. Each color will represent a species and each piece will represent an individual. (For example, you are an individual and so is every other person you know. All people are members of the same species, which is called Homo sapiens. Therefore you represent one individual (among 6 billion) of one species. Now make up a "community" of paper squares, (which represents a community of animal species) by combining paper squares of different colors and varying numbers of individuals. For example:

| Color (Species) | Pieces (Individuals) |
|---|---|
| Red | 30 |
| Black | 15 |
| Green | 9 |
| Brown | 8 |
| Blue | 6 |
| Yellow | 4 |
| Orange | 2 |
| White | 1 |
| Total | 75 |

The community above has 8 species (species richness is 8) and 75 individuals.

Put all the paper squares into a box or large can and pick out a square, only looking at it after you have taken it out of the box. Write down the color of the square and return it to the box. Now pick out another square, record the color and return it to the box. Continue this until a sample of five pieces has been recorded. What is the number of species found so far? Now pick five more pieces, returning each to the box after you pick, and add the results to the previous sample. Now how many species have you found? Pick ten more. What happens to the total number of species recorded? It gets larger.

This means that the diversity you find in a sample will get larger if you pick a larger sample. So now we have three different samples of the same community and three different diversity values (species richness) because each sample is a different size (sample sizes of 5, 10 and 20 individuals). Did you find all eight of the species in your samples? Probably not. In real life, you never truly know the diversity of a community until you have counted every individual.

## Comparing diversities

Biologists often want to compare diversities between different environments (like comparing a tropical rain forest with a temperate rain forest) or see how the diversity of an environment has changed over time (Is the diversity of the city park less now than it was 30 years ago?). Likewise, a paleontologist might want to know the diversity of an environment before and after extinction.

Suppose you are a biologist and you want to know if the animal diversity of the wetland near your house has changed in the last 50 years. You fence off an area so that no animals can get in or out, and you spend all day catching and counting every animal in that area. At the end of this process, you have recorded 209 individuals and 15 species. You then go to the library and find that in 1942, a biologist took a sample of 43 individuals and found 13 species. At first you might think that the sample taken in 1942 was less diverse, but your sample is more than twice the size of the 1942 sample, and you have already seen how sample size can affect your diversity measure. How can you compare these differently sized samples? There is a simple equation that allows us to compare diversities from different sample sizes. It is:

$$S-1/\text{Log } N$$
Where S = number of species and N = number of individuals in the sample.

If we apply this equation to the problem above we find that your sample of 15 species and 209 individuals works out to:

$$15-1/\log \text{ of } 209 = 14/2.3 = 6.5 \text{ species}$$

Now apply the equation to the 1942 sample of 13 species and 43 individuals:

$$13\text{-}1/\log \text{ of } 43 = 12/1.6 = 7.5 \text{ species}$$

Therefore, the 1942 sample, which only has 13 species, seems to represent a larger community than the recent sample, which has 15 species.

## Another aspect of diversity

There is more to diversity than just the number of species in an environment. A community that has more or less equal numbers of individuals of seven different species will look more diverse than a community that is dominated by one species. Try this activity to illustrate the effects of differing proportions of individuals on diversity.

Using your paper squares, make up two "communities" like these:

| | Community 1 | Community 2 |
|---|---|---|
| Red | 42 | 8 |
| Black | 1 | 8 |
| Green | 1 | 8 |
| Brown | 1 | 8 |
| Blue | 1 | 8 |
| Yellow | 1 | 8 |
| Orange | 1 | 0 |
| | 48 individuals | 48 individuals |
| | 7 species | 6 species |

Put each "community" into a coffee can or box and mix them up and then dump them onto a table top into separate piles (Figure 7.5).

Which community looks more diverse? Community 1 does not look very diverse because most of the squares are red. Community 2 looks more colorful, and therefore more diverse, even though it has a lower species richness. Think about it this way: Imagine each color is a different food; red is a hotdog, black is an egg, etc. If each community represents

## FIGURE 7.5

Visual depiction of the pieces of paper representing two communities.

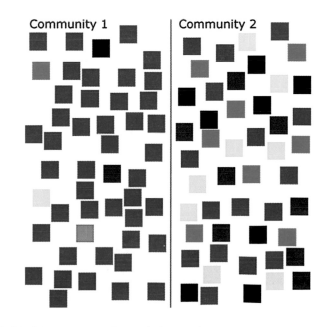

your menu, which will seem less diverse? When all the species of a community are represented by nearly equal numbers of individuals, we usually think of that community as being more diverse than one where one species is very abundant and dominates the environment (even if the second community actually has more species). Because of this, some measures of diversity include a way of counting the number of individuals of each species as well as the total number of species. One commonly used measure of species diversity that includes proportions of individuals is represented by the Shannon-Weaver equation, which is:

$$H(S) = -\Sigma\, p\, i \ln p\, i$$

where $p\, i$ is the proportion of species "i" in the community and ln is the natural logarithm. The table below illustrates how this is calculated.

|  | p i | ln p i | p i ln p i |
|---|---|---|---|
| Sample 1 | 0.90 | -.0105 | -0.095 |
|  | 0.04 | -3.219 | -0.129 |
|  | 0.03 | -3.506 | -0.105 |
|  | 0.02 | -3.912 | -0.078 |
|  | 0.01 | -4.605 | -0.046 |
|  | S= -0.453 | H(S)= 0.45 |  |
| Sample 2 | 0.46 | -0.798 | -0.367 |
|  | 0.26 | -1.347 | -0.350 |
|  | 0.16 | -1.832 | -0.293 |
|  | 0.09 | -2.408 | -0.218 |
|  | 0.03 | -3.506 | -0.105 |
|  | S= -1.33 | H(S)= 1.33 |  |
| Sample 3 | 0.20 | -1.600 | -0.320 |
|  | 0.20 | -1.600 | -0.320 |
|  | 0.20 | -1.600 | -0.320 |
|  | 0.20 | -1.600 | -0.320 |
|  | 0.20 | -1.600 | -0.320 |
|  | S= -1.600 | H(S)= 1.60 |  |

Each sample above represents 100 individuals. The first column represents the proportion of individuals for each species (Sample 1 has 90 individuals of the first species, 4 individuals of the second, etc.). The second column represents the log of this number and the third column represents the product of the first two columns. Note that even though all three samples have the same number of species (five) and the same number of individuals, they have widely different Shannon-Weaver diversity indices. The evenly distributed Sample 3 has a much higher diversity that the very dominated Sample 1. We call Sample 1 dominated by one species and Sample 3 equitable.

## Differences in diversity between environments

Species diversity is often used as a measure of environmental health. For instance, an oil spill will typically cause diversity to drop both in terms of numbers of species and equitability. A stressed environment will typically have a low number of species, with one or two of these species dominant in numbers of individuals. Species diversity also tends to increase along environmental gradients such as temperature and salinity. Tropical environments are more diverse than cooler ones and fully marine environments are more diverse than brackish ones, all other things being equal.

# Fossils in Society

Fossil fuels (coal, oil, and natural gas) make up over 80% of our energy sources. They are called fossil fuels because they all come from ancient organic matter that has been buried and then heated over a long period of time. These fuel sources take so long to form that they are not renewable and there is much discussion now as to what will replace them when they, especially oil and natural gas, are expended. Activity 1 (Coal, petroleum, and natural gas) describes the origins and processes of formation of the fossil fuels and guides students in an investigation of the properties of coal and its younger brother, peat. Activity 2 (Making thin peels of coal balls to view ancient plants) examines the actual plant fossils in coal balls and makes an important link between fossils of the past and our energy needs today.

Topic: Fossil Fuels
Go to: www.scilinks.org
Code: AP019

# Coal, petroleum, and natural gas

Today, our main energy sources are the solid coal, the liquid petroleum, and the gas methane. What will take the place of these three fuels in the future is anybody's guess. But for now, coal, petroleum, and methane are the royal family of energy minerals. See how they compare with each other, with nuclear energy, and with renewable energy sources, such as hydroelectric, solar, and wind. See Figure 8.1.

The numerical amounts for each form of energy in Figure 8.1 is in quadrillion BTUs. Thus, domestic energy from coal, petroleum, and natural gas in 2001 in the United States was 58.38 x 10 BTUs. Add to that 8.7 x 10 BTUs for nuclear and 6.03 x 10 BTUs for renewables and you get a total of 72.48 x 10 BTUs for domestic production. Take that number and add the amount of energy forms that were imported (30.45 x 10 BTUs) and you have the total energy supply for the United States in 2001 of 100.23 x 10 BTUs.

FIGURE 8.1

U.S. energy flow for 2001.

**U.S Energy Flow, 2001**

**Source:** Energy Information Administration. U.S. Dept. of Energy. *Monthly Energy Review.* August 2002: in quadrillion BTUs

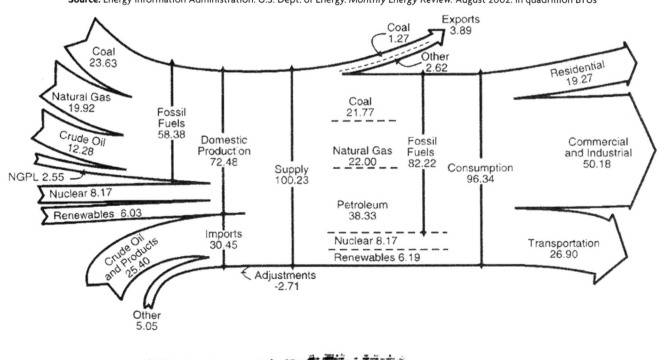

The U.S. exported 3.89 x 10 BTUs, which leaves 96.34 X 10 BTUs for consumption. The public used the energy in three ways: residential (19.27 x 10 BTUs), commercial and industrial (50.18 x 10 BTUs), and transportation (26.90 x 10 BTUs).

Coal, natural gas, and crude oil are called **fossil fuels.** Coal came from extinct and ancient land plants that died and fell into swamps. Gas and oil originated from microorganisms that lived in the sea or fresh water and settled to the bottom at death and did not rot in the stagnant water.

If the vegetation falls into the swamp and immediately is covered by the deep water, the plant materials will not rot, but will begin the long process of turning into coal. If an entire tree falls into a stagnant swamp, the tree sinks and little of the tree will rot. At first, the plant material becomes peat, then it compresses to lignite, then under continuous pressure, changes to bituminous coal, and finally becomes anthracite coal. The original mass of peat will compress to less than 1/25 of its original volume. In the Carboniferous Period of the swamps, a reasonably pure coal could be produced if a little sediment accumulated in the swamp at the same time.

Oil and methane also come from organic material, but it is not as clear as the origin of coal. Petroleum comes from marine sediments. Dark organic-rich shale is the probable source. The Black Sea is accumulating mud that is 35% organic, compared to the mud in the Atlantic Ocean with an average of 2.5% organic material in ordinary sediments. In normal marine sediment the organic material is oxidized, but in stagnant bottom water it can accumulate. The situation is very similar to the formation of coal. As with coal's deep burial, much time and some heat are required to make oil and gas. Once formed, it must migrate to permeable rock from which it is extracted. Not all oil forms in marine rocks. The oil shale of the Rocky Mountains area, which contains a large percentage of our petroleum resources, formed in freshwater lakes, probably by the same process.

Obtain some samples of peat, lignite, bituminous coal, anthracite coal, and coke.

1. Look for fossil plant life in the fossil material.
2. How has the fossil plant material changed as it became older?
3. Coke is made by heating coal in a container by a process called destructive distillation, driving off the volatile gas and leaving the carbon in the container. The carbon coke has many uses, one of which is to pull oxygen out of metal in a refinery furnace. This can be demonstrated in the laboratory.
4. How well do the different types of coal fuel burn?
5. How do bituminous and anthracite coal compare in weight, hardness, luster, flame, and as a fuel?

# Making thin peels of coal balls to view ancient plants

## MATERIALS:

- coal balls which have been sawed in half
- #400 grit (carborundum abrasive)
- glass grinding plates
- hydrochloric acid, 5% by volume
- acetate film .003 inches thickness (cellulose acetate)
- acetone
- scissors
- water
- dissecting microscope

## Objectives for this activity are:

1. To understand what a coal ball is, how it forms from a mass of vegetation, and how it was preserved about 250-350 million years ago,
2. to learn the acetate peel technique, and
3. to use a dissecting microscope to examine acetate peels for the structure of ancient plant tissues.

## Introduction

During the Carboniferous Period, about 250–350 million years ago, plant material which fell to the swampy forest floor decayed, became compacted, and turned into the amorphous substance which time, pressure, and heat transformed into coal. Some of the plant material, however, became saturated with $CaCO_3$ and other salts, which filled the interior of, and area between, the cells. As this hardened to stone, the cellulose of the cell walls was preserved and embedded in limestone. This limestone concretion, the coal ball, is formed in coal seams and constitutes a nuisance to mining operations. Discarded by the industry, the preserved material comprises an important key to understanding the detailed structure of carboniferous plants. Evidence gathered from coal balls assists paleobotanists and systematic botanists as they explore relationships among extinct and modern plants.

Joy, Willis, and Lacey (1956) published a simple method of obtaining peel from coal balls. Their acetate peel method is shown below in five steps.

## The Acetate Peel Method

1. Sprinkle a few drops of water and small amount of carborundum grit on the surface of the glass grinding plate. Grind the cut surface of the coal ball on the plate with a circular motion for 15–30 seconds. Then wash the coal ball surface with water.
2. Etch the surface of the coal ball by holding the cut and freshly ground surface in an acid bath containing 5% HCl for 15–20 seconds. (This process dissolves the calcium carbonate from the cut surface, leaving the cellulose of the fossil cell walls exposed and somewhat fragile. From this step to the end of the process it is necessary to avoid touching the cut surface, as the cell walls that are raised can be easily damaged. Wash the surface with a stream of water from a wash bottle, thus stopping the action of the acid. Allow the etched surface to dry for about 20 minutes.
3. Cut a piece of acetate film approximately 5 centimeters longer and wider that the coal ball's surface. Level the surface of the coal ball and use a wash bottle to flood the surface with acetone. CAUTION: Acetone fumes are highly inflammable. This should be done in a room where there is adequate ventilation and there are

## FIGURE 8.2

Acetate peel of a coal ball.

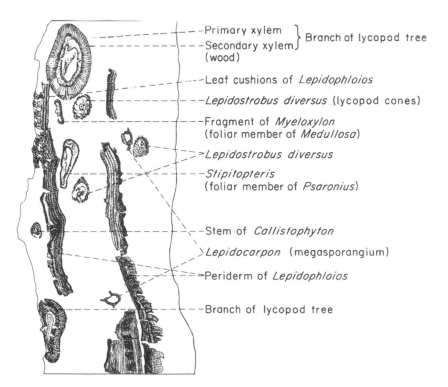

no sparks! While acetone is still standing on the surface, slowly roll the acetate film onto the coal ball.

4. Allow the acetate film to dry for at least 20 minutes. A peel may be left in place overnight or longer without harm. When dry, carefully peel the acetate film away, and trim the rough or uneven edges. Store the peels in envelopes or paper clipped to an index card. Examine the peels under a dissecting microscope. Figure 8.2 shows an example of a peel. Figure 8.3 identifies several of the major plant components of the coal ball in Figure 8.2.

5. For each successive peel, it is necessary to obtain a fresh surface by grinding a new surface as in step 1. As only a small amount of material is removed with each successive peel, it is possible to use each coal ball repeatedly. Thus, a single coal ball slice can remain in an interest center over a long period of time, or a classroom set of several coal balls can serve a whole class, taking turns throughout the week.

## FIGURE 8.3

Identities of the major plant components of the peel in Figure 8.2.

Primary xylem  
Secondary xylem (wood) } Branch of lycopod tree

Leaf cushions of *Lepidophloios*

*Lepidostrobus diversus* (lycopod cones)

Fragment of *Myeloxylon* (foliar member of *Medullosa*)

*Lepidostrobus diversus*

*Stipitopteris* (foliar member of *Psaronius*)

Stem of *Callistophyton*

*Lepidocarpon* (megasporangium)

Periderm of *Lepidophloios*

Branch of lycopod tree

## Sources of Materials:

Plant Fossil Microscope Kit
(Kit containing fragment of a coal ball plus materials for making 12 acetate peels).
Available from:
Carolina Biological Supply Company
Burlington, NC 27215.
Tel 919-584-0381 or 800-334-5551.

**Cellulose Acetate Film, 003″ thickness.** Available in rolls from:
Dick Blick
P.O. Box 1267
Galesburg, IL 61401
Tel 309-343-5785 or 800-373-7575.

**Coal Balls:**
Coal balls can be picked up at many strip-mining sites in the United States.
They are also available from:
Ward's Natural History Science Establishment
5100 West Henrietta Road
Rochester, N.Y. 14691-9012.
Tel 716-359-2502 or 800-962-2660.

## References:

Joy, K. W., A. J. Willis, and W. S. Lacey. 1956. A rapid cellulose peel technique in paleobotany. *Annals of Botany* 20 (80): 635–637.

Ma, P. R. 1992. Thin peels of ancient plants. Presentation at Annual convention of National Science Teachers Association, Boston.

Philips, W. N., M. J. Avcin, and D. Berggren. 1976. Fossil peat from the Illinois basin: A guide to the study of coal balls of Pennsylvanian age. Illinois State Geological Survey Series 11.

# When Are Fossils Art?

Whenever a fossil is beautiful, appealing, or is more than of ordinary significance, it may be called art. Some critics will find a fossil fascinating, while others see just a boring rock. There are aesthetic standards when a fossil is more beautiful, more appealing, or of more than ordinary significance. These standards are the criteria that determine whether a fossil has the emotional quality to inspire the viewer to perceive something in it that is dramatic. The immensity of *Ultrasaurus macIntosh* may be shown by including just the four extra long legs to scale in a grove of trees in a park. The dance of the two images of Jurassic shrimp in split rock, turned upside down, appears to be human performers.

Two activities on fossils in art are in Chapter 9. In the first, the student is challenged to submit an entry on dinosaurs to a campus art contest for an outdoor art display somewhere in its extensive environment. Thirteen criteria guide the student. The total cost for the materials, set-up, and the prize is $40,000.

The second activity involves fossils that can be displayed in a form that catches the eye. The display should encourage the viewer to wonder about color, shape, beauty, symmetry, odd footprints, or density. Fossils can be spectacular in innumerable ways. Can you suggest a fossil that will make an amulet, an ornament for your living room, or an image on a T-shirt?

SCI LINKS
THE WORLD'S A CLICK AWAY

Topic: Dinosaurs
Go to: www.scilinks.org
Code: AP020

# Dinosaur art contest

For about 170 million years, the dominant group of organisms on Earth were the dinosaurs. At least, that is what scientists tell us... and the media (books, journals, TV, and news press) constantly interprets every new morsel of facts the scientists uncover. From the reign of dinosaurs only a mere 350 species have been identified. Thousands of species of dinosaurs more are thought to have populated Earth, but for some reason they haven't been found yet. *Seismosaurus*, measuring 150 feet from mouth to tail tip, and a *Brachiosaurus* that towers at 55 feet high have been found, but there are probably thousands of smaller extinct dinosaur species not yet discovered.

So much has been written about the dinosaurs—and so very much more is unknown about them—that stories about their size, behavior, reproduction, extinction, and care for young fascinates us.

You might try sponsoring a Dinosaur Art Contest. Students can design a sculpture for display on the campus of a school or university.

## Suggested criteria:

◆ The sculpture should be dinosaur inspired.
◆ You may select a wooded area, an open area, or a combination of the two.
◆ The size should be less than 50 feet square and less than 65 feet high.
◆ The sculpture can be real or abstract.
◆ It can be fashioned of any material: wood, stone, concrete, metal, or clay.
◆ It can depict a part of a dinosaur, one individual, a population, or a community.
◆ It should convey information, emotion, or beauty to the viewer.
◆ That message should be unforgettable—stay with the viewer forever.
◆ It could affect awe, humor, pity that they are no longer alive, or relief that they are extinct.
◆ You do not need to have artistic technical skills, but you do need to be inspired.
◆ Be original.
◆ Title your sculpture.

See Figure 9.1 for an example of Dinosaur Art.

# FIGURE 9.1

Example of the reconstruction of a dinosaur in its natural habitat.

# Fossil works of art

Fossils are often considered works of art. They can sometime startle you with their beauty. They provide a peek at the past, of things and events seldom seen or imagined today. They are lifeless, but some show their last struggle for life. They are mathematically fashioned in a symmetry of coils, screws, or boxes. They may inspire a human characteristic in an inverted shrimp "dancing" across a piece of Solenhofen limestone 150 million years ago. Or one fossil may be the most beautiful Trilobite you have ever seen.

## FIGURE 9.2

*Glossopteris* ferns from the Carboniferous Period.

## FIGURE 9.3

Trilobite from Cincinnati, Ohio.

These pages show some photographs of fossils that have artistic elements.

Figure 9.2 is a split rock in black and white of fossil *Glossopteris* ferns from the Carboniferous Period 360 to 290 mya. The two split rocks open the sandwich of white fossil enabling one to see the part and counterpart images of the fossil leaves. It's like looking at both the finger and the fingerprint of the fossil.

About 500 million years ago, on the floor of a muddy sea near present-day Cincinnati, Ohio, trilobites skittered around on the impressionable mud. Their tracks hardened in the mud, were buried for half a billion years, and in the 20th century appeared at the surface of a streambed (Figure 9.3).

Black dense rock shaped by tumbling water and gradually filled with now white coral (Figure 9.4). It's very heavy. That's about all we know about it. We put it on a table and people ask two kinds of questions: What is it? How did it form?

## FIGURE 9.4

Fossil coral in black rock.

## FIGURE 9.5

Agatized leg bone from the Cretaceous of Patagonia.

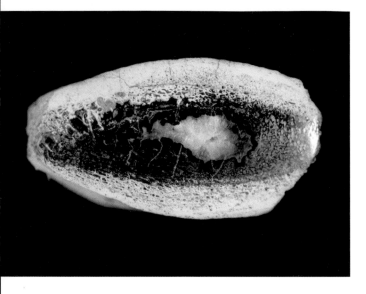

A cross section of a leg bone that fossilized during the Cretaceous Period in Patagonia, Argentina (Figure 9.5). The densest portion of the outer surface of the bone was replaced by a white form of agate, the less dense bone was infiltrated by red agate (red jasper), and the open space in the center of the bone was filled with colorless quartz. The impregnation of white, red and clear quartz is a natural coincidence for the colors of the tissues.

The ammonites (such as those in Figure 9.6) were the most symmetrical and colorful animals that lived in seas during the Mesozoic Era. Like the dinosaurs and the pterosaurs, the ammonites became extinct some 65 million years ago. What could have happened to these fashionable jewels of the sea?

## FIGURE 9.6

Cut and polished ammonites.

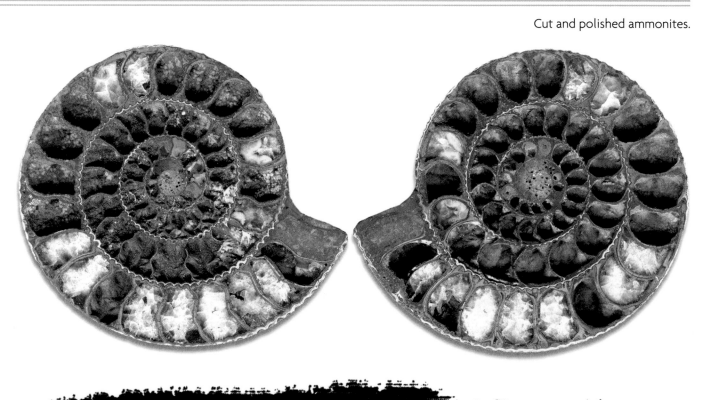

**Age of the Earth.** Meteorites are remnants of the original material of the solar system and have an age of approximately 4,600,000,000 years.

**Age of Reptiles.** The four geological periods, Permian, Triassic, Jurassic, and Cretaceous (280–65 million years ago), during which reptiles were the dominant animal on land and in the surface water of the sea. Recently, the subclass of Archosauria (the dinosaurs, pterosaurs, crocodiles, and birds) has been raised to a Class separate from reptiles.

**Amber.** A fossil resin secreted by healthy tropical flowering and conifer trees in response to wounds inflicted by boring insects or mechanical injuries.

**Archosauria.** A proposed class of vertebrates containing the dinosaurs, the crocodilians and birds, and certain extinct forms.

**Archaeopteryx.** The earliest bird found in Jurassic rock in Germany. So far there are ten specimens with half dinosaur and half bird characteristics.

**Aves.** Formerly the class name for birds, which now appear to be dinosaurs specialized for flight.

**Biped.** Two footed as Homo sapiens, birds, and some dinosaurs.

**Carbonization.** A fossil that has been reduced to a carbon scale, as a leaf that has been preserved as carbon.

**Cast.** A fossil that forms as minerals in a space previously occupied by a living specimen.

**Cenozoic Era.** The current time zone dating back to 65 million years known as the Age of Mammals.

**Cladistics.** The goal of cladistics is to place organisms in a sequence of space that corresponds to the tree of life. To accomplish this each species is selected on the basis of the simplest distribution of derived characteristics to approximate the historical branching of the tree of life.

**Coal balls.** When coal forms some of the material becomes saturated with calcium carbonate and forms into round concretions of rock and fossil material. Discarded by the mining industry, the concretions are valuable fossils representing 250–350 million year old forest plant life with preserved cell structures.

**Continental drift.** The theory that land masses move across the face of the Earth on mobile crustal plates.

**Copal.** Amber that has not yet been hardened by seawater. Can be detected by jabbing it with a hot needle.

**Crater.** A scar made by a body colliding with Earth, sometimes miles or millimeters in diameter.

**Cretaceous Period.** The latest period of the Mesozoic Era, 144–65 million years ago.

**Dinosauria.** A subclass of the Archosauria comprising the Orinothischia and Saurischia.

**Dinosaur Art.** An object depicting an aspect of dinosaur life that evokes an emotional response.

**Displacement.** When a model dinosaur is immersed in water it takes the place of an equal volume of water. If the volume of displaced water is measured it is equal to the volume of the model.

**Diversity.** Given the population of a community, the numbers of species that make up the total population of that community constitutes its diversity.

**Ectothermic.** "Cold-blooded," having a variable internal temperature, dependent on external conditions.

**Egg nests.** The nest sites of communal dinosaurs are found in large groups and may have been protected from predators on islands. The nest sites give evidence that the dinosaurs provided care for the young.

**Eighteen-inch layer.** In the Green River Formation of Wyoming there is a layer of fossiliferous rock that is 18 inches thick and that has a superabundance of fish fossils of all sizes and species. It is thought that at this time there was a series of significant fish kills.

**Endothermic.** "Warm-blooded," having a constant internal temperature independent of external conditions.

**Evolution.** A change in the genetic characteristics of a population of organisms over a series of generations brought about through natural selection.

**Extinction.** The death of an entire species.

**Fossil.** Traces of organisms in rocks preserved by geological processes.

**Fossil fuels.** An energy source of heat that was captured by the sun in plants. Includes the solid coal preserved in swamps, the liquid oil from plants and animals preserved mostly deep in the ground, and the natural gas preserved in porous rock in the ground.

**Fossil works of art.** Fossils that have the special quality to evoke emotions in the viewer.

**Forests of coal swamps.** The swamp trees and other vegetation that form the forest plant community during the Carboniferous Period and contributed coal.

**Geological time scale.** Whereas we use a clock and calendar to track events in our daily lives, the geologist uses a time span of the age of Earth, 4,600,000,000 million years, to track the events of the Earth. The scale is divided into Eras (e.g. Mesozoic) and Periods (e.g. Cretaceous) and Epochs (e.g. Miocene) and finally Ages (e.g. Maastrichtian).

**Homology.** The fundamental similarity based on common descent. The vertebrate humerus, for example, is present, or was present in the embryo, in all vertebrate animals from amphibians to humans.

**Joules.** The Standard International unit of energy equal to the energy done by a force of one newton when its point of application moves a distance of one meter in the direction of the force. It is equivalent to 10 erg or one watt-second.

**Jurassic Period.** The middle Period of the Mesozoic Era, 208–144 million years ago.

**Linnean System of Classification.** A classification in which all species of organisms are grouped in nested boxes from species, genus, family, order, class, phylum and kingdom based on overall similarity. The thought was that this grouping would reflect the sequence of evolution of life.

**Mammals.** Hairy animals that suckle their young. They emerged late in the Permian Period, but were suppressed by the archosaurs throughout the Mesozoic Era, and emerged as the dominant land animal during the Cenozoic Era.

**Mass extinction.** The death of large numbers of species due sudden changes in the environment.

**Mesozoic Era.** The age of archosaurs from 245–65 million years ago.

**Microfossil.** A fossil so small that it can be only identified and studied with a microscope.

**Micrometeorites.** Dust-like meteorites that enter the Earth atmosphere continually as shooting stars, they may be shaped like microscopic spheres or small irregular solids.

**Mold.** The imprint of something like teeth bitten in a block of clay. Filling the mold with plaster of paris would produce a cast.

**Paleobiogeography.** The study of the distribution of ancient plants and animals and their relationship to ancient geographical features.

**Permian Period.** The last time period of Paleozoic Era (286–245 million year ago) characterized by dry land and the early domination of reptiles followed by the emergence of mammals.

**Permineralization.** Pores of the skeleton of the organism, such as bone or wood, are filled with minerals. Most petrified wood is preserved in this manner.

**Phytoplankton.** Microscopic plants floating at the surface of bodies of water throughout the world. Responsible for photosynthesis, which fuels the aquatic system.

**Pterosaur.** One of the flying archosaurs whose wings were composed of leather airfoils supported on a single little elongated finger.

**Quadruped.** Four-footed as horse, salamander, and some dinosaurs.

**Radiation.** A process in which the descendants of a successful species diversify in function and form to occupy more than one niche.

**Replacement.** The process of a molecule-for-molecule exchange of one substance for another. For example, the shell of a mollusk might be replaced by pyrite.

**Reptiles.** A class of terrestrial vertebrates including lizards, snakes, turtles, and their extinct relatives. Reptiles are ectotherms with three chambered hearts. They were ancestral to mammals and archosaurs.

**Sedimentary rock.** Mineral or organic matter deposited by air, water, or ice and forming a layered deposit.

**Scientific theory.** A well-established science explanation for natural phenomena that has been tested many times and not been proven wrong.

**Species.** The major subdivision of a genus regarded as the basic category of biological classification, composed of related individuals that resemble each other and are not able to breed with other species.

**Strata.** Layers in sedimentary rock or anything else.

**Taphonomy.** The circumstances and processes of fossilization.

**Taxonomy.** The science dealing with the description, identification, naming, and classification of organisms.

**Trace fossil.** A fossilized track, boring, burrow, trail, or other structure in sedimentary rock that records the organism or behavior of the organism that made it.

**Triassic Period.** The first period of the Mesozoic Era, 245–208 million years ago.

*Ultrasaurus macIntosh.* The largest dinosaur fossil discovered. It was found in Jurassic rock in Colorado, and is believed to have weighed an estimated 150 tons.

**Vertebrate.** Animal with backbone, e.g., fish, amphibians, reptiles, archosaurs, mammals, and birds.